IDOLeyes

IDOL*eyes*

my new perspective on
FAITH, FAT & FAME

MANDISA

WITH ANGELA HUNT

Tyndale House Publishers, Inc.
Carol Stream, Illinois

Visit Tyndale's exciting Web site at www.tyndale.com

Find out more about Mandisa at www.myspace.com/mandisa

TYNDALE and Tyndale's quill logo are registered trademarks of Tyndale House Publishers, Inc.

American Idol® and the *American Idol®* concentric oval design are registered service marks of FremantleMedia North America, Inc., Burbank, California. All rights reserved.

*Idol*eyes: *My New Perspective on Faith, Fat & Fame*

Designed by Jacqueline L. Noe

Edited by Susan Taylor

Published in association with Yates & Yates, LLP, Attorneys and Counselors, Orange, California.

Library of Congress Cataloging-in-Publication Data

Mandisa, date.

   Idoleyes : my new perspective on faith, fat & fame / Mandisa with Angela Hunt.

      p. cm.

   Includes bibliographical references.

   ISBN-13: 978-1-4143-1602-4 (hc)

   ISBN-10: 1-4143-1602-X (hc)

   ISBN-13: 978-1-4143-1603-1 (sc)

   ISBN-10: 1-4143-1603-8 (sc)

   1. Mandisa, date. 2. Christian biography. 3. Spirituality. 4. American Idol (Television program) I. Hunt, Angela Elwell, date. II. Title.

   BR1725.M26A3 2007

   277.3′0825092—dc22

   [B]   2007009800

Printed in the United States of America

14 13 12 11 10 09 08
7   6   5   4   3   2   1

DEDICATION

I am indebted to a group of people who have been a great support to me throughout my journey on *American Idol*. Some of them are my closest friends; I know them like the back of my hand. Some I may recognize only by face. And still others I have never met. But at one point or another, all of them have lifted my name to the heavenly Father in prayer. I could try to name you all, but that would be impossible. So to be sure I include each of you, I dedicate this book to the body of Christ. I consider it an honor to be called your sister. I love you.

There is one body and one Spirit,
just as you have been called to one glorious hope for the future.
There is one Lord, one faith, one baptism,
and one God and Father,
who is over all and in all and living through all. . . .
He makes the whole body fit together perfectly.
As each part does its own special work,
it helps the other parts grow,
so that the whole body is healthy and growing and full of love.
EPHESIANS 4:4-6, 16

CONTENTS

FOREWORD

I couldn't sit down. Not even during the commercial break leading up to the moment each week when Mandisa would take the stage. Neither could I bring myself to go to the houses of friends who were popping popcorn and watching the show en masse. I was too nervous. And anyway, I needed to concentrate; God forbid that anyone would talk when I was trying to listen. This was big, and I didn't want to miss a single facial expression on that screen. I held my cell phone in a choke hold in my left hand. I'd need my right hand to throw something at the television if one of the judges had the audacity to be derogatory. The cell on the left, however, was the necessity. Anybody who knew the drill knew to let her fingers do the talking the second the lines were open. After all, this is the land of the free and the home of the brave, where the democratic process of getting to cast your vote is an inalienable right.

The phone was stuck to me like glue for a few other reasons as well. I often had some kind of text message from Mandisa on broadcast days, directing me how to pray. I also needed to be ready to text my buddy Travis Cottrell at least half a dozen times during the course of the show. He has been the worship leader for our Living Proof Live events for nearly a decade and is the one who introduced that precious woman into my life. Our girl was in a world none of her advisors had ever navigated. In fact, had the decision been up to some of us, we probably would have counseled her to stay under the umbrella of the church at large and out of the harsh elements of a mean world. It wouldn't have done any good. To her tremendous credit, if Mandisa believes God has told her to do something, there ain't no mountain high enough.

I remember the first time I ever laid eyes on Mandisa. I was meeting my team at an arena in Charlotte, where we were holding an event for the next twenty-four hours. I am the lone Texan serving with a mass of Tennesseans, so I'd flown in separately, getting my notes ready and keeping my face turned to the sky, seeking a torrential downpour of God. I had worked with the same basic praise team for several years, and I was wild about every single one of them. We have truly been a team in every sense of the word, never seeing ourselves as two separate entities on that platform. Worship is very important to me. The Word is very important to them. I'm in the front row while they lead the singing. They're in the front row while I lead the study. We do what we do *together*.

Travis had let me know we had a sub on the worship team that weekend in Charlotte. One of our regulars had not been able to make it. The thought that Mandisa came to us as a sub still amuses me. It just goes to show, God doesn't call subs. There are no accidents in His work. There is no coincidence in who backs out and who steps up. He moves His chess pieces around the board at will, and that weekend, we got the queen.

When we gathered for prayer time before the event began, I still hadn't heard her sing, but I instantly liked her. Mandisa has a sweetness in her demeanor that is endearing before you know how gifted and stunning she is once the cat is out of the bag. In that small room in the underbelly of the arena, I sat across from her for the first time and had to fight the temptation to stare at her. My goodness, she was beautiful. Not only that, she was dramatic. Goodness knows, I like a little drama. I can't remember if she prayed out loud with us in our first prayer time or not, but once she did, I marveled over the depth of relationship I could tell she had developed with Jesus at such a young age. I recall thinking that she must have known a lot of pain to love Him like that already. Only in the Christian faith is desperation a gift.

As our praise-team novice took the platform that evening, she'd learned forty songs in three days, complete with sign language to one of them. She was a team player. And when it was her turn to take the lead, she brought the house down.

Travis loves to shock me. If he has somebody new on the team and he knows full well the person is going to blow my mind, he usually won't tell me in advance. He waits until I'm standing in the front row with my chin to the ground, having a near-death experience, before he cuts his eyes away from the keyboard and laughs his head off at me.

Not long after that, Mandisa became part of the family. We have had the great honor of serving alongside that darling young woman of God many, many times over the years that followed. Travis summed it up beautifully: "In all my years of doing this thing, there was never one any more musically prepared, more 'prayed up,' and more selfless in their offering." She had a huge gift without a huge ego. What an incredible rarity!

Mandisa was not only a wonderful worship-team member. She was also a remarkable student. A teacher's dream. A lover of Christ and a devourer of His Word. She had remarkable insight and the gift to express it. She was dead honest about her issues and dead-on about the solutions. I have no idea how many times I quoted something she'd said backstage in her feedback on a lesson, and it never failed to resonate deeply with the participants. Then came the time in Seattle, when we actually handed her the microphone and let her express to the audience for herself what God had been doing in her heart. I was flabbergasted. *You have got to be kidding me,* I thought to myself. *The woman can sing* and *speak?* Yep, apparently she could. Who ever said life was fair? Travis reminded me how we all piled in the van after that event with exactly the same thing on our minds: We, a consummate group of loudmouths, were dumbstruck. I broke the compulsory moment of dead silence with a prophetic word: "I think *we* are all going to be working for *her* before it's all over." And lo and behold, look at us now. It took a maniacal card game of Pit in the hotel that night for our team to recover.

I love Mandisa Hundley. I've cheered for her so many times that I've nearly thrown my back out. So maybe you can imagine how devastated I was when I felt responsible for an unfair and public attack made on her values after she sang a blatantly Christian song on *American Idol.* Her critics didn't have grounds for the attack based on anything she had said. They tied her to me and held her responsible for some of my stands. We were both floored. Mandisa wouldn't offend a flea if she could keep from it, and I've spent my adult lifetime trying to love and serve anybody God puts in my path, regardless of differing beliefs. I'd been called a lot of things, but never a hater. As for Mandisa, until then, I don't think anyone had ever had an unkind word to say about her. They still wouldn't have if they'd known her. The worst part of the ordeal was seeing her labeled unfairly because of me. My heart broke. I felt I'd hurt a friend I'd so wanted to support. I wept before the Lord and said, "Look what I did!"

God responded in a way I didn't anticipate. I felt Him say clearly in my heart, "Look what *you* did? *You?* I believe *I* wrote the Book. You'd better look at what *I* did. And what great things I'm going to do."

God has only begun to use Mandisa Hundley. He put her to the test, and she passed it. Her faith proved genuine in a world that esteems pretense highly and rewards it richly. Even when a number of Christians would have preferred that she be less vocal about her faith until she had bagged the prize, she took her moment in the spotlight and gave it to Jesus. Maybe she agreed with something my grandmother from the hills of Arkansas used to say: "You betta dance with the one who brung ya."

That night Mandisa threw the shackles of expectation off her feet so that she could dance. And I'd be willing to bet that she had an unseen Partner: One who can take her far beyond any platform this world can offer her.

If you haven't had the pleasure of knowing her already, I am honored to introduce you to my friend Mandisa. When you turn the last page of this book, I think you'll be nuts about her. There's still room on that dance floor in case you want to join her.

—Beth Moore

PROLOGUE

On a chilly January night in 2006, I gathered with twenty of my closest friends to watch my first appearance before Simon Cowell, Randy Jackson, and Paula Abdul, the judges for *American Idol*. I smiled and tried to remain calm, because I knew something no one else was supposed to know. I had done a pretty good job of keeping quiet, but most of my friends had taken one look at my shining eyes and guessed my secret—I'd made it past the round that would be televised that night. In a few minutes I would sing for America; then the judges would hand me the coveted "golden ticket" and tell me that I could advance to the next level of competition.

That wasn't all they'd said that day. As soon as I had finished singing, Paula said, "You definitely have the pipes."

And Simon said, "You were everything I'd hoped you'd be." Simon, known for his brutal evaluations, had also commented on my pretty face.

The three judges looked at each other, smiled, and then together counted: "One, two, three—you're going to Hollywood!"

I was so excited when I left the room that when host Ryan Seacrest asked how I felt, I'd said, "This feels like *heaven!*"

Those golden memories colored my thoughts as I smiled and chatted with my excited friends. Someone had lit candles throughout the room, and the dining table was practically groaning from all the food on it. A party atmosphere filled the house, and I was having the time of my life.

In order to avoid the commercials, my friends and I were watching *American Idol* on TiVo, but other friends in Nashville were watching in real time. I was confident of the night's outcome—after all, I'd already *lived* through the hard part—so I didn't think it the least bit odd when the phone rang and Chance, the party's host, stepped away to answer it.

A few moments later Chance caught my eye and motioned to me. I stood and walked toward him, wondering why the joy had fled from his expression. I wanted to celebrate, but Chance looked as if someone had just died.

"Mandisa—" he pulled me away from the others—"Kevin just called. They're watching the show live."

I blinked, unable to understand the reason for the shadows in his eyes. I knew I'd made it past the panel of judges. I'd already been to the next round in Hollywood, so he couldn't tell me it had all been a mistake.

"Simon," Chance said simply. "After you left the room, he made comments about your weight."

I looked away as my eyes filled with tears. Simon? Though more than a few *Idol* contestants had felt the sting of his tongue, he'd been complimentary after I sang. He'd agreed that I should go to Hollywood . . . and he'd said I was pretty.

I closed my eyes and felt myself slipping back to high school, where immature, rude boys had called out cutting comments when I performed with the drill team.

I thought I'd heard the last of cruel and callous remarks. But I was about to hear them again, with twenty of my closest friends nearby to witness my humiliation on national television.

I'd have run away if I could. But big girls don't run, even if they do cry.

I waited patiently for the Lord *to help me,*
    and he turned to me and heard my cry.
He lifted me out of the pit of despair,
    out of the mud and the mire.
He set my feet on solid ground
    and steadied me as I walked along.
He has given me a new song to sing,
    a hymn of praise to our God.
Many will see what he has done and be amazed.
    They will put their trust in the Lord.

Oh, the joys of those who trust the Lord,
    who have no confidence in the proud
    or in those who worship idols. . . .

Lord, *don't hold back your tender mercies from me.*
    Let your unfailing love and faithfulness always
    protect me.
For troubles surround me—
    too many to count!
My sins pile up so high
    I can't see my way out.
They outnumber the hairs on my head.
    I have lost all courage. . . .

But may all who search for you
    be filled with joy and gladness in you.
May those who love your salvation
    repeatedly shout, "The Lord *is great!"*
As for me, since I am poor and needy,
    let the Lord keep me in his thoughts.

Psalm 40:1-4, 11-12, 16-17

1 Waiting Patiently

Hello. I'm Mandisa, and I'm a foodaholic. I'm also addicted to reality television. I love cheesecake, ice cream, and *The Amazing Race.* My idea of a perfect night is an up-sized cheeseburger meal deal followed by a two-hour episode of *Survivor.*

These days I'm learning how to deal with my food addiction, and I'm choosing to eat healthily. I've come to realize that being overweight is bad for my body and that if I'm going to be a good steward of the life God has given me, I need to change my eating habits.

The reality shows, however, are a different story. God has not led me to give those up; instead, He's used them to change my life.

Before I ever thought about auditioning for *American Idol,*

I had watched every episode of every season and knew all the finalists by name. I believe *Idol* is the greatest TV show in the world, and every time I watched, at the back of my mind lurked a question: *What would happen if I were to audition?* But whenever I'd wonder about my chances, I immediately reminded myself that I was too old. For the first three seasons, contestants could be no older than twenty-four when they auditioned, and I was twenty-five when *Idol* first aired in the United States.

Ultimately, though, I'd flash back to all the comments I'd heard Simon make to people who are overweight—let's face it, the man is not the sort to spare anyone's feelings. He must adhere to the philosophy that one must be cruel to be kind, because I've seen him deflate dozens of contestants' hopes with a well-placed barb.

Still, I couldn't help but wonder. Then, at the start of season four, *Idol* raised the age limit to twenty-eight. I was eligible . . . but I didn't have peace about proceeding. The timing didn't feel right.

Yet as I celebrated my twenty-eighth birthday in October 2004, I realized that would be my last year to be eligible for an *Idol* audition.

Was I going to let fear of one man's comments keep me from fulfilling a dream? Would I blow out the candles on my thirtieth birthday cake and wonder if I could have qualified for the competition?

In the early winter months of 2005, I decided that I wanted to live a life of no regrets. I didn't want to reach thirty-five or forty and still be wondering whether I had what it took to make it onto the *Idol* stage.

Back to the Beginning

I grew up in Citrus Heights, California, near Sacramento. I lived with my mother, Ruby Hundley, and spent every other weekend with my father and stepmother, John and Millie Hundley.

My parents named me *Mandisa*, which means "sweet" in the language of the Xhosa, a South African people group. Growing up, I heard my name pronounced every imaginable way. Kids used to tease me by calling me "Medusa," so I'm sure you can understand why I wasn't thrilled to be compared to an ugly mythological monster with snakes for hair. Because of that horrible nickname, in junior high I tried to change my name to "Kandie." After all, *Mandisa* means "sweet," and what is sweeter than candy? On the first day of school I would approach my teachers before class and tell them that I wanted to be called Kandie instead of Mandisa.

The result? Many of my classmates never knew what my real name was. When I enrolled in junior college, I finally decided it was time to let go of my childhood nickname and live under the name my parents gave me.

There's power and meaning in a name. And just as my friends struggled to switch from calling me "Kandie" to calling me "Mandisa," I've had to learn how to refer to my mother by a different name. In 2003, Mom decided that she wanted to return to her maiden name, Ruby Berryman. My brother, John, and I were grown, so she wouldn't have to explain why she and her children had different last names. I also think she wanted to clear out some painful memories from the past.

Like most children who grew up with divorced parents, I felt torn between my mom and my dad. I wanted to love them equally, but it's not easy to be loyal to both parents when they

3

are divided by hurts that are as tender today as they were thirty years ago.

Like millions of working mothers, my mom was out of the house most of the day, so I spent many nonschool hours at home in front of the television. Combined with my love for food, those periods of inactivity began to pack extra pounds on my childish frame. In hindsight, I can understand why researchers have discovered that children who watch more than three hours of television a day are 50 percent more likely to be obese than kids who watch fewer than two hours. In fact, more than 60 percent of instances of being overweight can be linked to excess TV viewing.[1]

I started getting heavy in late elementary school, and there I heard my share of fat jokes and sharp comments. Kids can be cruel, and even though I had always recited "Sticks and stones may break my bones, but words will never hurt me," I would have preferred any number of broken bones to the sting of those condemning words.

Yet I could forget those mean remarks and nicknames when I went home and lost myself in a TV show. I'd go to the refrigerator or cupboard, grab a snack, and settle down on the sofa as I ate and laughed and let the television take me away from the real world.

When I wasn't watching TV, I'd go to the bathroom, pick up a curling iron, hold it like a microphone, and watch myself in the mirror as I sang along with the radio and pretended I was a talented television star.

Lately I've come to understand that I'm an introvert by nature. I used to think that introverts were shy and withdrawn, and I enjoy parties and people! Now I understand that being an introvert means that I need to be alone to reenergize. I suppose it's because of that tendency that I've always preferred sedentary activities to active ones. As I grew heavier, the excess pounds only reinforced my preference. My personality, combined with the ridicule I sometimes heard, led me to stay indoors and keep to myself.

I might have continued forever in a sort of vicious cycle—eating and sitting, sitting and eating—until a new interest entered my life by way of a book.

A Novel Leads the Way

My high school creative-writing teacher assigned the classic novel *Stranger in a Strange Land,* by Robert A. Heinlein. Michael Valentine Smith, the hero of Heinlein's novel, is a human raised by Martians. He comes to earth as an innocent child, grows up, establishes a church, preaches love, and ultimately dies—the fate of most messiahs.

The book is pure science fiction, yet because it is filled with spiritual symbolism, it piqued my interest in God. The Lord began to woo me, His Spirit drew me, and I responded.

I don't want you to think I'd never been taught anything about God. My dad and stepmother went to church, but since I saw them only twice a month, church wasn't a regular part of my life. God wasn't a top priority for me, but thankfully, I was a top priority for Him.

Now I can see how God shaped events in my life to draw me to Him. On my sixteenth birthday, instead of asking for a car or the latest trendy outfit, I asked for a Bible. My friend Jennifer Bradshaw, a Christian, was eager to provide one for me. I thanked her and planned to read that Bible from cover

> God wasn't a top priority for me, but thankfully, I was a top priority for Him.

to cover, but when you don't know the Lord and you don't understand what you're reading, the task can get a little daunting around Leviticus and Deuteronomy.

I eventually set the Bible aside, but God didn't give up on me. Two months later, a coworker of my mother's invited Mom and me to go to see the "Singing Christmas Tree" at her church. The three of us filed into a pew, and I don't think I blinked more than a half dozen times as the music and narration told the story of Jesus. I had heard the story before, but this time I felt something different. Since the story hadn't changed, I suspect something in *me* had changed.

My heart warmed as I watched Mary place the baby Jesus in the manger. Tears welled in my eyes as Jesus hung on the cross and begged the Father for mercy. Terror gripped me when I saw a frightening portrayal of hell and the devil. Joy leaped in my soul as Jesus ascended to heaven on what I assume were cables being manipulated by men backstage. I knew the actors were volunteers reading lines of a script, but their performance provided answers to several of the questions I had about Jesus. My heart had been hungering for knowledge, and that church drama fed my soul.

When the music ended, the pastor stood and explained that the story I had seen was a reenactment of actual events. Jesus was a real person. He was God's Son. He came to earth to save us—to save *me!*

The pastor read from the Bible and explained that since we are all sinners and no one is perfect, a relationship with Jesus is the only way we can reach heaven. When the pastor asked, "Would you like to know Jesus tonight?" I felt a stirring in the pit of my stomach.

The pastor continued: "While everyone bows their head

and closes their eyes, if you want to meet Jesus, quietly repeat this prayer."

When he prayed, I prayed with him. I told Jesus I believed everything I had just seen on the stage. I was lost, and apparently He was in the business of helping lost people get found. I also confessed that I didn't want to go to hell, because it looked like a scary place. If He would accept my life, I would give it to Him and let Him be my Lord, my boss, from that day forward.

Then the pastor surprised me. I'd been thinking I could sit in the pew and give my life to Jesus quietly, but the pastor said, "If you prayed that prayer, raise your hand so we can all know about it."

> I was lost, and apparently Jesus was in the business of helping lost people get found.

Lifting my hand took every ounce of courage I possessed, but I did it. I was nervous, because my mom was sitting next to me. She'd been raised in church, but she didn't attend anymore. What would she think if I lifted my hand?

I raised my right hand, the arm nearest the aisle, thinking that maybe she wouldn't notice what I was doing. Then the pastor surprised me again. "Now," he said, "if you've lifted your hand, come down here so we can give you some material."

Gulp. Mom was sure to notice if I stood up and left the pew. For an instant I hesitated; then I realized that following through with Jesus was the most important thing I could do in that moment. So I stood and walked down the aisle, met the pastor, and took the material he gave me.

As I read the material, I learned that following Jesus is a day-by-day process of growth and learning. While Jesus accepts us the moment we accept Him, nobody becomes "Super Christian" the moment they meet Jesus.

I was no exception.

Church Meets a Need

Let us not neglect our meeting together, as some people do, but encourage one another, especially now that the day of his return is drawing near.

HEBREWS 10:25

For someone who's decided to follow Christ, church attendance is important, because that's one place we can learn about God and spend time with other believers. I wanted to go, but I didn't have a way to get to church. Mom still didn't attend, and we didn't have enough money for me to buy a car. So nearly two years passed between the time I accepted Christ and the time I was able to go to church.

The first Sunday after I got my license, I drove my mom's car to Genesis Missionary Baptist Church. I had sung at a Martin Luther King Jr. event a few years back, and many of the organizers of the program attended that church. But to be honest, I chose Genesis because I had a crush on the young man who played drums for the church!

Thankfully, though, I loved everything about Genesis Missionary Baptist Church. At the end of the service, when the pastor asked people to come down if they wanted to become a church member, I stepped out of the pew and strode down the aisle with the determination of a quarterback. As the other members—including my drummer friend, Kevin—came up to hug and welcome me, I felt as accepted and loved as if I'd been part of that church family all my life.

From that day forward I began to dig deep to discover what following Christ was all about. No one had to remind or nag me to attend services; I was *starving* for knowledge about the Lord and what the Bible says about the way we should live.

After graduation from high school, I moved to Nashville to attend Fisk University (a Historically Black College/University). At school I met others who were following Christ, and I began to attend a small campus Bible study led by my new best friend, Chandra.

She was so patient with me and my questions. She had grown up in the church and was so knowledgeable about the ways of God. I, on the other hand, was a mere baby in the faith and inquisitive by nature. Through the good teaching at the Bible study, I became desperate to know Jesus better. I began to listen to music designed to glorify Him; I began to read books that took me deeper into spiritual topics and lessons.

As I matured, I began to understand that the path of the Christian life is not paved with stardust and flanked with smiling faces—it's a path of struggle, and sometimes it leads to suffering. But there are blessings in the struggle—and, yes, even in the suffering.

> As I matured, I began to understand that the path of the Christian life is not paved with stardust and flanked with smiling faces—it's a path of struggle, and sometimes it leads to suffering. But there are blessings in the struggle—and, yes, even in the suffering.

As I talked to Chandra and others about Jesus and His purpose for our lives, I wondered about His plan for me. What was I supposed to do with my life? All I had ever wanted to be was a singer, but was that what Jesus wanted for me?

I didn't have any other remarkable talents. In elementary school I tried to play the flute but decided that ethnic lips just weren't meant to pucker that way! In junior high I switched from the band to the choir, but it wasn't until high school that I felt validated as a singer.

In fact, my life took a major turn in high school, even before I decided to follow Christ. I entered El Camino Fundamental High School with a group of friends I'd known in junior high. We began to hang out with a group of people who were morally questionable. They drank, smoked, and stole from others.

In an attempt to be accepted by them, I, too, began to steal. I would go into the girls' locker room while the class was in PE and rifle through purses and bags that were kept in an unlocked locker. I knew it was wrong, but I felt "cool" doing it.

I was headed down a dangerous path and could have ended up in jail if not for a teacher who took notice of me. My high school choir director, Mr. Robinson, noticed my love for singing and worked with me to build my confidence.

In my freshman year, Mr. Robinson asked me to sing "You'll Never Walk Alone" for a state competition. I was terrified of the high note right before the end, but Mr. Robinson spent hours outside class giving me voice lessons and working with me to perfect my performance. I did improve during those weeks of rehearsing, but by the time of the competition, I still felt mediocre. The judge who evaluated me, however, said I had a great high voice, and his positive feedback did a lot to boost my confidence.

From that point on, I became a different person. I stopped hanging around with the crowd that had dragged me down and began spending time with people in choir and drama. I became more active in the performing arts department and took classes in music and drama.

Mr. Robinson and my drama teacher, Lee Elliott, saw something in me I didn't see in myself. From my sophomore year on, they cast me in the lead roles in all the musicals: In tenth grade I played Paulette DePaul in the musical *Over Here.* I was Golde in *Fiddler on the Roof* in my junior year, and in twelfth grade I was privileged to play Princess Winnifred in the musical comedy *Once Upon a Mattress.*

I began to see myself as a performer, and with my teachers' encouragement ringing in my heart, I practiced and concentrated on my singing. I realize now that many people are born with a musical voice—I don't remember ever *not* singing. But my talent grew as I learned more about my vocal instrument and how to use it.

While Mr. Robinson and other teachers were teaching me how to breathe correctly, sight-read music, and sing from my diaphragm, I thought it was a waste of time. Now, however, I use all of those skills on a regular basis. When gifted young singers ask me where to begin, I highly recommend participating in choir, competitions, music-theory classes, and even piano lessons. The skills developed in those activities can give you an edge in a world where good singers are a dime a dozen.

After high school I continued to learn more about my

instrument at Fisk, where I majored in music with a concentration in vocal performance. I continued performing, too, even playing Effie in the college production of *Dreamgirls*. I loved the feeling of being onstage and drawing people into the dramatic world I was helping create. I began to believe that God had created me for performance.

After graduation, however, I wasn't sure what I was supposed to do with my voice. I knew that many famous musicians made a comfortable living with their music, but how does one go from being a "graduate with a degree" to "famous musician"?

The Lord had a plan, although at first I couldn't see it.

If There's a Will, Is There a Way?

Trust in the LORD with all your heart; do not depend on your own understanding. Seek his will in all you do, and he will show you which path to take.

PROVERBS 3:5-6

When I graduated from Fisk on May 24, 2000, the world seemed bright and promising. The next day, however, I woke up and realized that I had a college degree but no money, no job, and no place to live.

Chandra and her roommates let me crash at their place while I sorted through my thoughts. I was thankful for my bachelor's degree in vocal performance, but it was not exactly the kind of credential that results in a variety of career choices.

Some time ago a friend told me about her new car's GPS device. I listened in amazement as she explained how the Global Positioning System on her dashboard receives signals from at least four GPS satellites in the sky. The signals enable it to calculate the car's position in three dimensions. I'm still not sure how it all works, but when the voice on my friend's GPS device says, "Turn right in thirty feet," you can bet she does. She doesn't even need to look at a map, because the automated voice allows for her mistakes and quickly directs her back to the right road.

After my graduation from college, I trusted the Lord to direct my path like some sort of heavenly GPS system, but I hadn't heard a word about my destination—or even my direction. The screen on my internal GPS was completely blank. I needed direction, and I needed it fast.

At the time I was working through *Experiencing God,* a Bible study by Henry Blackaby. Because Blackaby talks about being aware of what God is doing around us, I was looking for situations where God was working so I could join Him. One day, after finishing my reading, I closed the book to spend some time praying, but on the back of the book a logo for LifeWay Christian Resources caught my attention. I remembered visiting a LifeWay store with Chandra to purchase *Experiencing God,* as well as a study by a woman named Beth Moore. As I prayed, I felt a growing urge to go to the computer and look up LifeWay online.

My Internet search revealed that LifeWay was a company with Christian bookstores all over the United States and a corporate office located in Nashville, not far from where I was living. Furthermore, their Web site listed numerous job opportunities, including several in their music publishing department.

I sat back and felt a smile creep across my face. Surely my degree in music would qualify me for such a position. Surely *this* was the Lord's leading.

Greatly encouraged by this clear signal, I submitted an online application for no position in particular. Then I waited for the Lord to make His will clear.

In the meantime I received calls from several other businesses. I went to interviews and even received a few offers of employment, but I reluctantly turned them down because I felt certain the Lord had a job for me in LifeWay in a position that would utilize my degree.

Finally, my faith was rewarded. Someone from LifeWay called to schedule an interview, so I dressed up, went to the office, presented my credentials, and took the standard tests for evaluation.

A few days later I received another call. LifeWay was happy and pleased to offer me a job—in data entry.

The phone in my hand became as heavy as a lead brick. Was this some sort of joke? I was a university graduate! My classmates had entered the workforce as administrators, teachers, and program analysts. Surely LifeWay couldn't—the *Lord* couldn't—expect me to be happy about a position that required the mindless typing of numbers from Sunday school order forms!

But I had given my life to God. I had trusted Him to lead me, and He had control of the car—*and* the GPS, which was firmly directing me to LifeWay's data-entry department. After a long moment I drew a deep breath. Humbled, I took the position and trusted God. I settled into my cubicle and accepted the stacks of order forms, then typed them into the computer. Because the job could get tedious, I wore headphones at work, and as I typed numbers onto the screen, I sang along to the songs playing on my CD player. I must have sung louder than I realized, because soon I became known as "the girl in customer service who sings."

Because I was trusting the Lord, my contentment grew, and my spirit remained upbeat. That optimistic spirit, I think, had a lot to do with my being transferred from data entry to telephone orders and then to telephone sales. During the same span of time, I also progressed from singing along with the music in my headphones to singing solos in employee chapel services. I wasn't working in LifeWay's music department, but I *was* singing.

If the Lord Closes a Door, He Opens a Window

I will sing a new song to you, O God! I will sing your praises with a ten-stringed harp.

Psalm 144:9

Each spring, LifeWay holds a time of spiritual revival for its employees. They bring in a preacher and worship leader, and during my second year there, they asked a man named Travis Cottrell to lead the special music.

I had never met Travis, who in addition to many other events was also working as the worship leader for Beth Moore's Living Proof Live conferences. I had heard of Beth before I began working at LifeWay because I had completed *Breaking Free,* one of her Bible studies, while I studied at Fisk.

I didn't realize, however, how popular Beth's Bible studies were until I began taking telephone orders. After talking with excited customers, I learned about her LifeWay-sponsored women's conferences, for which Travis led worship. As the spring revival meetings grew near, I became excited about the chance to meet Travis, but I had no idea the events of that week would change my life forever.

Someone at the company had the bright idea of putting together an employee worship team to sing with Travis. They asked if I wanted to sing on the worship team. *Wow!* I was honored by the invitation and, if truth be told, a little intimidated.

15

I felt a bit out of my league when we began rehearsals and everyone knew all the songs but me.

When Travis realized that I didn't know the melody to "Come, Ye Sinners, Poor and Needy," he jokingly asked, "Are you sure you're a believer?"

In that moment, I knew I'd found a friend. That moment also forged the beginning of my relationship with the Beth Moore events. Travis called a few months later and asked if I would come to Charlotte, North Carolina, to sing on the praise team for a Living Proof Live event. I was thrilled by the opportunity, and as I packed for the trip, I realized that the Lord had begun to work in a surprising way. The car was rolling forward, but the GPS said only Charlotte, North Carolina.

In Charlotte, I stood on a stage in the center of an arena filled by fourteen thousand women. I had never sung in front of that many people before, and I was so nervous my throat kept going dry.

What if I messed up? What if Travis decided that I wasn't as good as he thought I was? What if those fourteen thousand women began throwing spitballs at me? My knees trembled as I walked onto the stage. Before we began what was supposed to be our first song, Travis leaned over and asked me to begin the event by singing "Amazing Grace"—all by myself.

For a second I thought about saying no. And I might have if Travis hadn't returned to his keyboard and struck the first chord to give me a starting pitch. The crowd fell silent, waiting.

With fear and trembling I mustered my courage and released a heartfelt version of the old hymn—a rendition that had never come out of my mouth before. The blood in my body began flowing again as Travis invited the ladies to join me in singing the first verse. As the event continued, we sang other hymns and choruses, and my spirit soared as I lifted my voice with others in praise and gratitude to my heavenly King and the One who had guided me to that place. I felt truly blessed and . . . at home.

Later I realized that God had begun to reveal His plan before my eyes. I continued to travel with Travis for various events, and eventually he asked me to sing on some of his worship CDs, an experience that introduced me to studio work. Producers and contractors became familiar with my name, and soon they were regularly calling me to sing on other studio projects.

Usually those projects involved my being one of sixteen singers recording a choral demo of new church musicals. Often I worked in the studio for relatively unknown artists working on their own CDs. Whatever the project, I was thankful for the opportunity to sing.

God and I were traveling down the highway together, and for a long while, I was content to work full-time at LifeWay and sing as the opportunities arose. Years passed before my soul grew restless and I found myself yearning for more.

A Simple Prayer

Oh, that you would bless me and expand my territory! Please be with me in all that I do, and keep me from all trouble and pain!

1 CHRONICLES 4:10

In the fall of 2002, my supervisor offered me a promotion within my department. The new job would bring in more money and give me more opportunity for ministry; plus, it was a position I'd been coveting for over a year. By that time, though, I knew not to assume anything about the Lord or His plans.

I needed His guidance, and I was desperate to know His

will. Several times in the Bible, I'd read about people who fasted—gave up food and drink for a set period of time—and prayed when facing an important decision. Moses, David, Jehoshaphat, and Ezra all fasted when they needed guidance, and the Lord gave them the help they needed.

Paul and Barnabas were praying and fasting with men from the church at Antioch. "The Holy Spirit said, 'Dedicate Barnabas and Saul for the special work to which I have called them.' So after more fasting and prayer, the men laid their hands on them and sent them on their way" on what was their first missionary journey (Acts 13:2-5).

At the beginning of Jesus' earthly ministry, right after His baptism, He fasted for forty days (see Luke 4:1-2). This intense time of focus and prayer gave him the strength he needed to withstand temptation and endure the trials of public ministry.

Abraham Lincoln called for a national day of fasting in America. His proclamation set apart Thursday, April 30, 1863, as a day of national humiliation, fasting, and prayer.[2] The Civil War was a dark time in our nation's history, but it ended slavery and restored our national union. God certainly heard the prayers of those who fasted and prayed for our nation.

I've heard it said that fasting is the direct opposite of man's first sin in the Garden of Eden. Instead of eating what is forbidden, as Adam and Eve did, a fasting person refuses to eat what is allowed. The purpose of a fast is to weaken people physically in order to strengthen them spiritually.

The Bible demonstrates that God honors an obedient child who sacrifices food for a while and instead uses that time to pray. There seems to be a correlation between emptying ourselves of things in this physical world in order to become more attentive to what God's Spirit wants us to hear spiritually. So before accepting the promotion at LifeWay, I fasted and prayed for three days. Then with great clarity and confidence, I declined the promotion.

While I was fasting and praying, I read *The Prayer of Jabez,* by Bruce Wilkinson. Influenced by Jabez's simple prayer, I asked the Lord to expand my territory and my circle of influence. Soon after I voiced this prayer, I received an invitation to go on a three-week tour called iWorship. I would be singing backup for established Christian artists Don Moen and Twila Paris.

As I thought about asking for time off so I could go on the tour, I began to sense that my time at LifeWay was drawing to a close. I wasn't sure what the future held—or even whether or not it held a steady paycheck—but I couldn't help feeling a sense of excitement. My path had forked: I could either stay where I was and enjoy the stability of a regular job, a consistent paycheck, and people whose company I appreciated, or I could take a three-week gig that might lead to something else—or to nothing at all.

For years I had made a regular habit of getting up and getting to the office early to spend some "quiet time" with God at the office. I knew that if I tried to do it at home, I'd probably fall asleep and be late for work. I remember sitting in my usual quiet corner at LifeWay and praying about whether or not to accept the tour invitation. I knew I could trust God with my future. I'd given Him my life years before, and He had never failed me. And I couldn't deny that I was excited by the thought of living a day-by-day faith adventure.

After telling the Lord that I would trust Him to provide for me after the tour, I went to my desk to begin work. One of my coworkers, Nelson Ray, walked up with an iWorship DVD and handed me the disc. "Here," he said. "I feel like the Lord is telling me to give this to you."

It was a small gesture, but it felt like a definite confirmation that I was doing the right thing.

With mixed feelings I said good-bye to my friends and co-workers at LifeWay. I will always be grateful for the things I learned there and for the way God used those people and that company in my life.

God calls people from some unusual places. His angel found "mighty hero" Gideon hiding at the bottom of a winepress (see Judges 6:11-12). David was a shepherd before he became Israel's most favored king, and Peter was a humble fisherman before he began fishing for people's souls.

Data entry? God knew that was exactly where I needed to be at the start of this amazing journey.

Full-Time Professional

The iWorship tour was a wonderful experience, but God used it as a sort of professional boot camp for me. For the first time in my life I was a full-time professional musician, relying on my musical ability and training to make my living.

On the tour I sang background vocals for Don Moen, Paul Baloche, and Twila Paris, as well as two songs with the worship team that travels full-time with Women of Faith events. Our tour consisted of fifteen concerts, and we spent most of our time in the northern and eastern parts of the country. I loved every minute of the experience, even the packing and traveling.

As an added benefit, once I came home, I discovered that I'd gained the connections and credibility to regularly land session work in Nashville recording studios. Talk about intimidating! During my first few outings I felt like a fish out of water among so many professionals.

For my first big job I was called into the studio to sing the guide and background vocals for an accompaniment track. I was so nervous that what was supposed to take a few hours actually took two days!

I quickly realized the work was harder than I had imagined. I would sing something and think it was okay, but when I listened to the engineer's playback, I could hear that I was either off pitch, off rhythm, or flat-out horrible! On those occasions I longed to be back sitting safely in my LifeWay cubicle.

But practice makes perfect. I hung in with the work and improved my craft as I learned from others. Most studio musicians have been doing session work for years. Instrumentalists can pick up a chart and play or improvise without a moment's thought; professional studio singers can sight-read almost anything the first time they pick up even a scribbled sheet of music.

At first I couldn't trust myself to record anything until I'd sung through a chart at least three times. While my fellow sopranos were confidently delivering their pitch-perfect notes, I would sing quietly until I got the hang of it. By the time I was ready to record, the group was moving on to the next section.

I knew it would take me a while to become confident at this work, but I was grateful for the opportunity because for the first time since leaving college, I didn't have a steady job. Yet between recording sessions and singing background for Beth Moore events, I managed to keep my bills paid.

I certainly wasn't living a luxurious lifestyle in those days. My one-bedroom apartment wasn't the Ritz, but it kept a roof over my head. My 1996 red Nissan 200SX had seen better days too.

I'll never forget the day I got that car. Although my father was not wealthy, he paid most of my college expenses from his salary as a federal civil servant. He also told me he would buy me a car if I got all A's during my sophomore year at Fisk.

When I presented him with my report card, Dad kept his promise and bought the car I ended up driving for eight years. That vehicle was a blessing in 1998, but by 2003, it was desperately in need of retirement. If I even thought about accelerating over sixty-five miles per hour, the engine put up a fit. The car that had gone from cute to clunker could barely wheeze down the highway, but it got me around town and helped me make ends meet.

The Lord was also blessing me in other ways. To my surprise, people began to ask me to lead worship for other events—on my own. My first reaction was, "I'm not a worship leader," and at first I turned several people down because I felt inadequate.

But when people kept asking—and knowing that the Lord often speaks through His people, the body of Christ—I decided I'd better consult Him to find out what He was up to. I asked; He answered: I was to lead worship. He would equip me; He would empower me.

What can you say when you hear promises like those? I took a deep breath and agreed to lead worship at a women's conference to be held at the First Baptist Church of Hendersonville, Tennessee.

I should explain that First Baptist of Hendersonville is a predominantly white congregation. They had invited me and an African-American speaker to address this conference. I was both excited by the opportunity and quaking in my shoes.

I've heard it said that courage is fear that has said its prayers, and I was "prayed-up" and ready to watch God work that weekend. I have always felt a burden for racial unity in the body of Christ—America is never more racially segregated than it is on Sunday mornings.

I love the promise found in Galatians 3:28: "There is no longer Jew or Gentile, slave or free, male and female. For you are all one in Christ Jesus."

In God's eyes, we are not black believers or white believers—we are His children, period. We are brothers and sisters, united in Jesus.

That weekend, as I stood before a sea of women representing all races, I felt the Lord's pleasure in us—and in me. Not because I was flawless; I wasn't. I was, however, desperate for Him and was depending on His power in my weakness. That day I caught a glimpse of His future plan for me. He had anointed me as a worship leader.

The experience reminds me of the words of a psalm:

> *I give you thanks, O LORD, with all my heart;*
> *I will sing your praises before the gods.*
> *I bow before your holy Temple as I worship.*
> *I praise your name for your unfailing love and*
>   *faithfulness;*
> *For your promises are backed*
> *By all the honor of your name.*
> *As soon as I pray, you answer me;*
> *You encourage me by giving me strength.*

PSALM 138:1-3

There's something amazing about the experience of using music to lead people into an awareness of the presence of God. There's no other feeling quite like it. When I'm singing worship music, the experience is not horizontal, solely between me and the audience. It's more vertical, between me and the Lord God.

In his book *The World Within,* Quaker philosopher and social reformer Rufus Matthew Jones said, "Worship is the act of rising to a personal, experimental consciousness of the real presence of God which floods the soul with joy and bathes the whole inward spirit with refreshing streams of life."[3]

He's right. And if I can use my music to ease world-weary people into the throne room of heaven, I am blessed indeed.

Nothing Ventured, Nothing Gained

My life had settled into a pattern by the fall of 2005. The Lord had proven Himself faithful, and I was happy doing session work. Yet I was still addicted to food and, on a less serious level, to reality television.

While watching the season-four *American Idol* finale with Carrie Underwood and Bo Bice, the question rose again in my brain: *What would happen if I auditioned?* Despite my fears, I couldn't seem to shake the feeling that I might be missing a real opportunity, so I made plans to go to the regional auditions scheduled for Memphis. That city was only a three-hour drive from my home in Nashville, so auditioning in Memphis wouldn't require a lot of time or money.

Because so many people audition for *American Idol* each year, many community media outlets sponsor regional competitions. They get extra publicity, and the winners of their contests are allowed to move to the head of the line at regular regional *Idol* auditions.

A Tennessee radio station sponsored a contest they called "Memphis Idol," so I sent in a CD that I'd recorded at my friend Kevin Perry's home studio. I was working on something else at

Kevin's studio when I saw an advertisement for the "Memphis Idol" contest. On a whim I threw together an a cappella version of the Jackson 5's "Who's Lovin' You" and mailed it in. But I never heard anything from the radio station, and a few weeks later Hurricane Katrina roared ashore and wreaked destruction along the Gulf Coast. Because tens of thousands of storm refugees poured into Memphis, the producers of *American Idol* decided not to put any additional pressure on Memphis city services.

They canceled the Memphis auditions.

I was disappointed, but not destroyed. Throughout the summer I had been telling myself that if I ran into roadblocks or closed doors, I would just drop the idea. I think the vulnerable part of me was still terrified of Simon Cowell and what he might say about my weight. The part of me that wanted to give everything to the dream of pursuing *American Idol* was constantly kept in check by the hurt little girl who'd heard too many mean comments in gym class.

I was certainly no stranger to mean comments. The object of my first real crush was named Joe, and while he wasn't a typical heartthrob, his short stature, black hair, and hazel eyes could put me in a trance.

Joe and I were in elementary school band together. He played clarinet, and I was still trying to contort my lips and play the flute. We made friendly with each other, and I became convinced that Joe had warm feelings for me, too.

The part of me that wanted to give everything to the dream of pursuing *American Idol* was constantly kept in check by the hurt little girl who'd heard too many mean comments in gym class.

Somehow I mustered enough boldness to write him a letter. Like so many other little girls, in closing I wrote, "Check yes if you like me and no if you don't." I folded the letter into a small box and adorned my masterpiece with happy-face stickers. I couldn't wait to give it to Joe.

Friday morning, before school began, I handed Joe the letter and ran away giggling, certain he would catch up to me at some point in the day. I passed the morning dreaming of what it would feel like to kiss my first boyfriend. Would he come up and hand me the letter with a big check mark next to the word *yes?* Or would he simply walk up and kiss me? Would the kiss be sweet—or slobbery?

The day ticked by slowly. When I hadn't received any response from Joe by lunchtime, I began to worry. By that time I was afraid to encounter him in person, so instead of going to the cafeteria for lunch, I went to the library.

But as I walked into the trailer that served as our makeshift library, Joe and his friend Corey stood by the librarian's desk. My eyes widened as the two of them smirked at me, and I whirled around to back out of the main door.

Amid a stream of giggling, I heard Corey's sarcastic taunt: "Joe doesn't like you. You're too fat!"

With two heartbreaking sentences, a boy destroyed my innocent hopes and dreams.

When the producers canceled the Memphis auditions, I wondered whether God was protecting me from the same sort of heartbreak and disillusionment. Was this my heavenly Father's way of preventing me from hearing, "Simon doesn't like you. You're too fat"?

Though I wanted to go out and follow my dream, it was easier by far to stay home, munch on my favorite snacks, and watch someone else's dreams come true on television in the comfort of my safe living room.

So when I never heard back from the radio station and the Memphis auditions were canceled, I assumed it wasn't the Lord's will for me to audition for *Idol*. I didn't think twice about it—until unexpectedly another door opened.

2 On Solid Ground

A couple of weeks after *Idol* producers canceled the Memphis auditions, I went online to do a little Internet surfing. I found an ad for another *Idol*-affiliated competition, a contest sponsored by Star 94 FM, Atlanta's WSTR. The radio station would determine the "Atlanta Idol," and the winner would receive airfare for two to the Chicago auditions, an overnight stay in a plush hotel, and admittance to the special line for contest winners. In other words, whoever won the "Atlanta Idol" contest wouldn't have to sleep in an arena or stand in line for hours waiting to audition.

I leaned closer to the computer screen to read the fine print. Unlike the Memphis contest to which I'd sent a CD, this contest asked entrants to call a number, leave a name and phone number, and sing into a telephone recorder for sixty seconds. That sounded simple enough.

I drummed my fingers on the keyboard, thinking. What did I have to lose? Absolutely nothing. So I dialed the number just to see what waited on the other end. I heard a voice thanking me for the call, then telling me to leave my name, number, and sixty seconds of a song.

I spent the next hour looking through my iTunes music to find the best song, then had to settle on the best *part* of a song. Most songs last three or four minutes, so I wanted to choose something that would showcase my range and voice—not always easy to do in only sixty seconds.

I chose Aretha Franklin's "Rock Steady," which is sort of an ironic choice, given the state of my nerves. Even though I knew the song inside and out, I spent another hour pacing through my apartment, practicing one section of the music over and over again. The tune was perfect for my voice; it was upbeat and fun, and it had some high notes where my voice would shine. I wanted my mini-audition to be *perfect*.

> After only about twenty seconds, I hit a high note—and the phone line went dead.

Finally I drew a deep breath and dialed the number again. I left my name and phone number first, then began to sing. After only about twenty seconds, I hit a high note—and the phone line went dead.

I didn't know what to do. Should I call back? Should I try again? For a moment I wavered; then I hung up my phone and backed away. What could I do about the phone cutting off? Not a thing. Memphis was canceled, the Memphis radio people either didn't get my CD or didn't like it, and now a hypersensitive answering machine had ruined my audition.

Obviously I was wasting my time and energy. *American Idol*

must not be part of God's plan for me. So why couldn't I give up and leave the idea alone?

An Unexpected Message

A couple of days later, on a Wednesday, I woke up a little earlier than usual. I lay in bed with the sun beaming through my blinds and directly into my eyes. I brought up my hand to shade my face, but out of the corner of my eye I saw a flashing light on my cell phone. I had a message waiting.

Who in the world? My friends knew that since leaving my nine-to-five job, I didn't roll out of bed until at least ten.

I grabbed my phone and dialed the code to retrieve my message. A cheery voice—a voice altogether *too* cheery, if you ask me, for eight in the morning—greeted me: "Mandisa, this is Kristen Gates from Star 94 in Atlanta. We'd like you to come down to our radio station and sing live on the air. You're one of six finalists in the 'Atlanta Idol' contest."

I sat up, as wide awake as if someone had just pumped me full of adrenaline. I screamed, not caring who could hear, because until that moment, I had convinced myself that the station's answering machine had erased my twenty-second entry.

I hurried to the phone and called Kristen's number. When I got her on the line, I confessed that I was surprised to hear from her since the phone had cut me off. She told me that they'd been having phone problems but that they were having *more* problems finding good singers.

"We want you to come to the station Friday morning," she said. "We're going to choose the winner on the air."

"Friday?" I glanced at my calendar. "As in the day after tomorrow?" I didn't want to say anything, but I'm not used to making spur-of-the-moment trips. My car had developed a couple of new rattles, and I wasn't sure it could survive the drive from Nashville to Atlanta without at least one breakdown.

Kristen wanted me at the station first thing Friday morning, which meant I'd have to drive to Atlanta Thursday night. I was scheduled to be in a Nashville recording studio all day Thursday, so how would I get to Atlanta? And where would I stay?

The scared little girl inside me had begun to talk me out of going before I even got off the phone. Was it really worth it? What if I got all the way down there only to lose to some perky, sixteen-year-old, size-two girl named Buffy?

Suddenly I longed for a side of bacon, scrambled eggs, and a stack of pancakes swimming in syrup and butter. Sweet and salty flavors would do the trick, and all that protein and flour would fill up the hollow place inside me.

The last time I'd had such a hearty breakfast, my college boyfriend and I had just broken up, and I was an emotional wreck. Our relationship ended in an argument about how far I was willing to go with him in the bedroom. He understood that I was not going to have sex with him because I believe the Bible makes it clear that sexual union is reserved for those who are married. But he couldn't understand that purity is about more than avoiding intercourse—it's about maintaining self-control and not arousing desires that can't rightly be fulfilled.

As much as I liked this young man, we were in two different places emotionally and spiritually, so we broke up. As I made my way back to my dorm, I stopped at Cracker Barrel, where they serve breakfast all day long. I sat down, placed my order, and drowned my sorrows in their Momma's Pancake Breakfast.

As I doubted my chance of becoming the Atlanta Idol, I

longed for "Momma's" pancakes to console me once again. I must have said something about not having a chance in the world, because Kristen abruptly commented that it would really be in my best interest to come down. Off the record, she told me, my chances were pretty good. I promised to try my best and said I'd call her later.

I immediately logged on to the Internet to see how much a flight would cost—and learned a valuable lesson. If you wait until two days before your departure to purchase a ticket, you'd better be prepared to pay a small fortune.

Despite my coupon cutting and frequent trips to the dollar store, I couldn't afford the flight, which would have cost about a thousand dollars. So I clicked on a page for rental cars and booked an economy car for one day. Transportation, *check*.

Next, accommodations. But this decision would prove to be a little trickier. My dad and stepmom lived outside Atlanta, as did my college roommate, Pamela Harris. I would have liked to stay with family, but the scared little girl inside me slammed the door on that possibility.

Like most girls, I have always longed for the unconditional love and approval of my father. My parents divorced when I was two, and within a short time my father married my stepmom. At the time of the Star 94 contest they lived about twenty miles from Atlanta in Fairburn, Georgia.

When I visited them as a child, I often felt like an outsider. I longed for Dad's affection and acceptance, and even though he loved me unconditionally, I didn't realize it. I thought love had to be performance based, so I assumed I could gain his love only when I could show him an A on my report card or announce that I'd won the lead in the school musical.

In 2003, my best friend, Chandra, and I took a quick trip to

West Memphis, Arkansas. We planned to meet her family at her high school alma mater for their homecoming game. Chandra had not seen her family for a couple of months, and I was eager to see them again as well.

As we drove to Arkansas, we talked about everything. We shared passages of Scripture the Lord had shown us in our quiet time, we discussed Old Testament prophecies, and we prayed together. It was so refreshing to talk about spiritual things with a friend.

As we climbed into the football bleachers, Chandra spotted her father cheering for the winning team. While I maintained my pace, Chandra picked up speed and sprang up the crowded steps. As I greeted her mom and sister, Chandra's and her father's eyes locked; then he stepped forward to embrace her. He hugged her for what seemed like hours, as if he were silently saying, *I missed you so much, and I'm so glad to see you. I don't ever want to let you go.*

As I made polite chitchat with Mrs. Allen, I couldn't help but think that I'd never had a hug like that from my dad. I knew that my mom and dad loved me, but I longed for the kind of relationship I saw between Chandra and her parents. They had been apart only a couple of months, yet they were as overjoyed to be together as if they had been separated for years.

I so wanted that kind of relationship, but I thought I would find it only with my heavenly Father.

As I considered where to stay when I visited Atlanta, the old performance anxiety rose in my mind, as powerful and nerve-wracking as ever. What if I went all the way to Atlanta and *lost* the contest? I couldn't face my dad as a loser. To tell the truth, I couldn't face *anyone,* but I needed a place to stay.

Fortunately, Pam, whom I jokingly referred to as my *room-*

dawg rather than my *roommate,* remained an option. Since the day we met at Fisk, Pam has been my biggest fan. She hadn't even heard me sing before she announced she just *knew* I would be a star one day.

If I lost the "Atlanta Idol" competition, Pam was the sort of person who would call the radio station and say they'd made a terrible mistake that they'd regret when I became a superstar. That's the kind of support I needed, so I called Pam and opened the conversation with, "Wassup, Roomdawg?"

I didn't tell anyone else about my impending trip. If I didn't win, I didn't want to have to tell anyone that I'd tried and failed. I didn't want to deal with sympathetic faces and consoling hugs. Better to lose quietly, I figured, than to build up everyone's hopes and then let them down.

I wasn't even sure I wanted to do that to myself.

You Want Me to Sing *What* Language?

Thursday seemed to drag as I stood in the Nashville studio and studied the music on the stand in front of me. That day proved to be particularly challenging—I was working with my friend Michael Mellett, but when I came in, I was surprised to learn that we would be singing in Japanese. Any other day, the challenge would have thrilled me, but that day I wanted to throw up my hands and scream in frustration.

Part of my brain listened to Michael and reminded my lungs and voice of what to sing; another part of my brain kept anticipating what would happen at the radio station in Atlanta on Friday morning. My imagination swirled with possibilities, both positive and negative, and I had a hard time focusing on my session work. I just wanted to be finished so I could get on the road.

I wondered if Michael sensed my agitation and distance. I wanted to explain and share my news, but instead I sang Japanese (or what I hope *passed* for Japanese) until six, when I was finally free to go home, load my rental car, and set out.

When I finally reached the highway, I had only Joyce Meyer and Kurt Carr for company. (I listened to a set of Joyce Meyer's teaching CDs and Kurt Carr's *One Church Project* worship CD on the drive.) Four hours later I arrived at Pam's house, feeling tired yet spiritually refreshed. I made it to bed by midnight but tossed and turned all night as "Rock Steady" played in my head.

Sleep was nearly impossible. Not only did I keep rehearsing my song, but I also kept trying to think of witty answers to questions they might ask. As I tossed and turned, each glance at the clock brought me closer to despair as precious sleep time disappeared.

At 3:45 I gave up on sleep. I tiptoed through Pam's house in the darkness while doing my vocal warm-ups—*me me me, ma ma ma, moo, moo, moo,* up and down the scale. While I warmed up, I got dressed and was meticulous with my appearance. Even though I would be singing on the radio, I knew that appearance matters on *American Idol.* So I worked with the curling iron to set every hair in place and applied my makeup as skillfully as I knew how.

The sun was still slumbering beneath the horizon when I went outside to join the thousands of commuters who drive in and out of Atlanta every morning. I had to be at the radio station by seven, and my stomach twisted into knots as I gripped the steering wheel and tried not to get lost while negotiating the unfamiliar traffic.

When I arrived at the Star 94 station, the little hope I'd been carrying within me shriveled like an old balloon. Five other finalists had gathered in the hallway—five young, hip, cool white people who all looked like models. They came with friends, parents, and well-wishers.

I felt as out of place as a bucket under a bull.

I didn't see how I could win. Unlike the others, I didn't even have an entourage. It took everything I had not to run out to that rental car and drive straight back to Nashville. But I'd come a long way, and I'd been up all night. Furthermore, no one but Pam knew I was there. If I bombed, at least I'd bomb in relative obscurity.

So even though I was the only contestant who'd come alone, the only heavy contestant, the only black contestant, and the only contestant over the age of twenty-one, I decided to go through with it. Aside from my pride, what did I have to lose?

I lifted my chin and took a seat with the others in a small kitchen area. The aroma of coffee swirled around us as DJs, staff members, and some of the other contestants' friends and family members helped themselves to coffee and bagels. Signs on the wall warned against leaving food out and not keeping the area clean.

> When I arrived at the Star 94 station, the little hope I'd been carrying within me shriveled like an old balloon. Five other finalists had gathered in the hallway—five young, hip, cool white people who all looked like models. I felt as out of place as a bucket under a bull.

One of the radio staff members had posted the order in which we would be singing, and I wasn't surprised to find myself last on the list. They could have listed me as performing next week, and I don't think I would have been any more nervous than I was in that hour. Maybe it was the lack of sleep, maybe a bad case of nerves, but I felt completely detached from everything going on around me.

Real and Imagined Fears

The odd feeling of separation reminded me of a weekend I had spent at my dad and stepmom's house as a little girl. On Sunday morning we got up early and headed out to Sunday school. We hadn't attended in several weeks, and since my stepsister, Vonnie, had moved up to an older group, I would be in a class where I didn't know anyone.

I walked into the classroom late and felt the hot pressure of a dozen pairs of eyes as the other kids turned to stare at me. My stepmom made sure I made it into the room; then she left to attend her own Bible class.

I looked for an empty desk and finally spotted one in the center of the room. I felt out of place and alone. Lowering my gaze, I nervously maneuvered through the maze of seats, then slid gratefully into the chair. Maybe if I sat still and didn't say anything, no one would notice I was there.

The teacher began to tell the day's Bible story. She talked about some guy named Jonah, a man who ran away and got on a boat with a bunch of strangers—*Who's that girl?*—before he decided to obey God. Then a big fish burped him up on the shore. And Jonah learned that he should always obey God.

You know her?

I didn't hear everything being whispered in that room, but I could imagine what the other kids were saying.

And my imagination rarely grants me any mercy.

That hour of Sunday school ticked by like Chinese water torture. I sat with my head down the entire time, afraid to look up and discover that the things I imagined were true.

As I sat in the lunchroom at the Star 94 radio station, I was tempted to revert to my childhood self and insulate my mind and heart with my oversized body. But I was no longer a child; it was time to grow up. So I made an effort to engage the others in conversation and tried to talk as freely as everyone else did.

As we talked, I learned that everyone else had listened to the other contestants' telephone entries. The recordings, including my twenty-second blurb, had been posted on the station's Web page.

My competitors had been busy researching. One of the guys, Adam, came up to me and said, "I just want to say good luck and I think you're the best!" His comment helped boost my wavering confidence.

While we waited, I drank lots of water. My throat was dry, and I liked holding the water bottle because it gave me something to do with my hands. But drinking all that water meant that I had to keep going down the hall to the bathroom.

Once, as I washed my hands at the sink, I looked into the mirror and wondered how in the world I had come to be standing in an Atlanta radio station. I felt different, intimidated, and out of place. I'd never been in that kind of environment. I'd done a lot of singing, but never under such competitive circumstances.

On my way back to the break room, I paused in the hallway and looked through a window that opened into the studio. I could see Steve and Vikki, the program hosts, with the two guest judges, a singer and a producer. The staff had gathered around a semicircular table and were laughing and talking, completely at ease though large microphones hung in front of their faces.

They finally lined up the contestants in the hallway, and

one by one they brought us in, had us sing, and conducted a brief interview. After every song, they immediately chimed in with encouraging comments.

I watched and listened as they interviewed the first young girl. One of them smiled at her and said, "Well, you certainly *look* like an American idol," and I thought it was all over. I might as well walk out.

At least I wasn't alone in my nervousness. Out in the hallway, almost all the other contestants were vocalizing, clearing their throats, or sipping hot tea. The parents present were in full helicopter mode—hovering over their kids, checking hair and makeup, encouraging the vocal warm-ups.

The atmosphere at the station was anything but comfortable. To add to the tension, we could hear the live broadcast through speakers on the wall. After each contestant sang, Steve and Vikki opened the phone lines so listeners could call in and comment.

I don't know if I've ever been more nervous. It's one thing to sing before a couple of judges and a few other contestants. It's quite another thing to sing before an unnumbered radio audience and invite them to call and say exactly what they think about your performance.

Occasionally one of the other DJs would walk out and talk to one of us for a promo spot, which only made me even more nervous. During these spot interviews I learned that all the other contestants were either high school or college students.

> It's one thing to sing before a couple of judges and a few other contestants. It's quite another thing to sing before an unnumbered radio audience and invite them to call and say exactly what they think about your performance.

The gulf between me and them widened as I told the interviewer I was a twenty-eight-year-old college graduate.

I felt as old as dirt and as big as a boulder. *Lord, are You sure You didn't make a mistake this time?*

Hold Steady

Finally the people in the studio called my name. I smiled and strolled in, trying to at least *act* confident. They asked me about living in Tennessee, and I said I'd found Star 94 on the Internet. They asked what I did for a living, and I told them I did session work. Then they introduced me and pointed in my direction.

There was nothing to do in that moment but sing. So I drew a deep breath and sang "Rock Steady." This time, at least, I was able to sing the entire sixty-second version I'd prepared, without any technical interruptions.

When I finished, I closed my eyes and waited . . . but no one spoke. I heard a silence louder than any high note I'd sung, and I dared to hope the silence was a good thing. If it wasn't, maybe I'd stunned them with sheer audacity.

Finally one of the judges remarked that I definitely would have made it if I had gone to the canceled Memphis auditions. "Amazing voice," he said. Another staffer beckoned me out into the hall, so I stepped out of the studio.

My fellow contestants greeted me with halfhearted applause. I leaned against the wall as my adrenaline rush faded away, leaving me weak-kneed.

Finished. I'd come this far and done my best. Nothing I could say or do now would make any difference at all.

While the station played a song by Usher, the staff conferred quietly, then rounded up all six contestants and herded us back into the studio. We stood there eying each other for a long moment, then Steve and Vikki announced that the Atlanta Idol would be . . . Mandisa.

I blinked—I think you could have knocked me over with a pinky finger. The judges asked me a few questions; I stammered out answers; then one of the judges said, "It's all about the voice. We couldn't have you not be the winner even though there were other factors involved."

He wasn't specific, but I knew what he meant. The American Idol is supposed to represent the complete package—the perfect look, sound, style, and showmanship. Without actually saying so, the Atlanta judges let me know that I'd won despite the "other factors"—namely, my weight. I didn't *look* like an American Idol, but as another of the judges said, "We couldn't get past the voice."

As I sat alone in the holding room completing a small stack of paperwork, a custodian came in to empty the trash. He looked surprised to see me sitting there, but he greeted me with a pleasant hello.

I glanced up and smiled at him as I filled out the necessary forms. The Hispanic man wore jeans and a flannel shirt with a work badge clipped to the pocket. Thick salt-and-pepper hair covered his head and filled in a generous moustache.

He looked up and caught my eye, then gestured toward the papers. "What are you working on?"

I cleared my throat and said I was filling out paperwork from the "Atlanta Idol" contest. I figured he had to know about the competition because the station had been promoting it for weeks.

His smile twinkled in his dark eyes. "Was it your daughter who won?"

I swallowed hard and chuckled despite a sudden quake in my self-confidence. "Um, I won, actually. I'm Mandisa."

The man blushed and offered a string of apologies. I laughed and told him I wasn't offended, but I also made a mental note—I didn't look like an American Idol. Apparently I looked like somebody's mother.

> I didn't look like an American Idol. Apparently I looked like somebody's mother.

I didn't let the thought bother me for long because by the time I had finished the paperwork and got back to my rental car, Pam had left five messages on my cell phone. I dialed her number and heard an echoing scream on the other line. Pam was so excited that at work she'd announced that her *roomdawg* was the next American Idol. Her boss got caught up in her excitement and let Pam leave to meet me at IHOP for breakfast. I was still yearning for those pancakes!

After pulling into the restaurant parking lot, I barely had time to get out of the car before Pam tackled me. She was screaming like a banshee, and I had to give her a few minutes to calm down before we could enter the restaurant.

I asked her to keep our little secret to herself—the victory was so new, I wasn't sure I believed it myself. I needed time to savor it before I could believe I had really won, but Pam didn't last five minutes. By the time we left, everyone in the restaurant had heard the name *Mandisa* and knew to vote for me come February.

While the sensible part of my nature knew I hadn't yet made it onto the show, Pam's remarkable faith in me gave me the confidence to tell my parents. I called my mom first, then my dad and stepmom.

While Mom's pride in me radiated through the telephone receiver, Dad's reaction wasn't exactly what I had hoped for. Rather than congratulate me, he was upset because I hadn't told him about the competition. He said he would have wanted to listen in and support me. I understood his disappointment, but at that moment, with Pam bouncing off the walls next to me, I wanted to hear that he was proud of me. With a lump in my throat, I explained what I was feeling, and Dad assured me that he *was* proud.

I followed up with calls to some of my closest friends. All of them were happy for me and proud of me. Most were upset because I hadn't told them anything before leaving town, but they understood why I'd been reluctant to talk about the risk I was taking. Something in me still couldn't quite believe I'd actually stepped out and taken the risk.

As I drove back to Nashville, I marveled at the miracle of everything that had happened in Atlanta. So many things had gone wrong before; so many doors had been closed. What was the Lord trying to teach me? Perseverance? Faith?

Maybe He was trying to urge me out of my shell. Maybe He wanted me to stop listening to the voice that urged me to remain in front of the TV with my comfort foods.

Maybe He wanted me to take more risks.

Little Girl Fears, Little Girl Dreams

When I was a child and people asked what I wanted to be when I grew up, the only answer I had to give was "a singer." As I grew older, people began to ask what I would fall back on if being a singer didn't pan out. I smugly replied that I did not plan to fail. I was going to be a singer—period.

But in college I began to question whether the dream of

singing was the Lord's—or mine. I had promised to live my life for Jesus, and I was willing to surrender that dream if my life could be spent in something that would please Him more.

I told the Lord I would be willing to bury my dreams for His sake, but after graduation I was still hoping to find a job that might utilize my musical training. When I accepted that Life-Way job in data entry, I thought God might be telling me that my dream was dead. As hard as it was to accept, I was okay with that—because accepting Jesus' lordship over your *life* means giving Him lordship over your *dreams,* too. I laid my desires at His feet, but a few months later I watched in awe as God began to resurrect the dreams I thought I'd given up forever. He placed me on praise teams; He gave me opportunities to lead worship. I could see the truth of Psalm 37:23: "The LORD directs the steps of the godly. He delights in every detail of their lives."

After winning the "Atlanta Idol" contest, I wondered where God was directing me next. I felt that the Lord and I had traveled the first few miles of an amazing adventure, but I didn't want to let my hopes rise too high. For one thing, that frightened little girl still lived inside me, and it's always easier to remain safe than to risk hurt. For another thing, I would truly rather be in the center of God's will than on any stage in the world.

> It's one thing to dream of being the American Idol when you're a young size-two girl or a six-pack guy—it's quite another to dream of that goal when you're big, black, and almost at the cutoff age.

And I couldn't help being practical. It's one thing to dream of being the American Idol when you're a young, size-two girl or a six-pack guy. It's quite another to dream of that goal when you're big, black, and almost at the cutoff age. Sure, some *American Idol* winners have broken through the stereotype (Ruben Studdard, winner of season two, was big, black—and beautiful, I might add!), but the majority of pop stars look more like Barbie and Ken dolls than like Cabbage Patch Kids.

Still, I couldn't help singing on the road from Atlanta to Nashville. I sang praise songs all the way home and let the Lord know I was willing to lay this dream at His feet. No matter what happened next, I was grateful to Him for bringing me this far and allowing me to experience this joy—and affirmation.

Next stop, Chicago—and I had only four days to prepare. I'd been nervous competing against five people in Atlanta, so how would I handle competing against thousands in front of Paula, Randy, and sharp-tongued Simon?

I would definitely have to be at the top of my game.

Once I got home, I did a juice fast and exercised every day, hoping to shed a few pounds before the audition in Chicago. I had not been disciplined with my eating in the weeks prior to the Atlanta trip, and I wish I'd known I'd soon be preparing for the audition of a lifetime. But it was too late for regrets, so I'd have to face the judges as I was.

In my ponderings, I was reminded of Ecclesiastes 11:4-6: "Farmers who wait for perfect weather never plant. If they watch every cloud, they never harvest. Just as you cannot understand the path of the wind or the mystery of a tiny baby growing in its mother's womb, so you cannot understand the activity of God, who does all things. Plant your seed in the morning and keep busy all afternoon, for you don't know if profit will come from one activity or another—or maybe both."

> If I failed . . . this time I would fail publicly.

I had no idea what to expect in Chicago, but I was finally ready to leave that little girl on the couch and take a major risk. I didn't know what God was doing, but I was ready to trust that He knew the way.

If I failed, though, this time I would fail publicly.

3 A New Song

By September 16, the day of the Chicago auditions, my nerves were as taut as violin strings. I flew to the Windy City from Nashville, and Pam, who was more than happy to accompany me, took a flight from Atlanta. We met at the airport and boarded a shuttle to the hotel generously provided by Star 94.

Among the others on that airport shuttle was a young man wearing a University of Tennessee Vols (Volunteers) T-shirt and a cowboy hat. His only luggage was a backpack with a rolled-up sleeping bag strapped to the top. When the driver asked each of us where we were going, the young man replied, "Soldier Field."

Pam and I glanced at each other and grinned. While that young, blond, buff American Idol hopeful rolled out his sleeping bag with thousands of other contestants at a stadium, Pam and I would be sleeping soundly at the Hyatt Regency McCormick Place.

We flew in the night before the *Idol* auditions so I could go to bed early and get a good night's rest. Before I headed to bed at eight, I spent some time praying, reading my Bible, and journaling. In my journal I wrote that I was still unsure of God's will in all of this. Was this my plan or His?

I had been disobedient to God by not eating well in the weeks leading up to this point, so I felt unworthy of God's favor. On the other hand, God's favor is unmerited—and He had a plan for me.

I wrote that I believed I would make it to Hollywood, then followed that statement with a question—*Would I?* But in my uncertainty, God provided support in the form of my friend Pam.

Just as Aaron and Hur held up Moses' arms during the battle against the Amalekites (see Exodus 17:10-13), Pam supported me whenever I wavered. I was so glad she had agreed to come with me to Chicago. I could have asked several people to join me on the trip, but after all of Pam's help during the Atlanta contest, I knew I wanted to ask her. She was a real cheerleader, and that's what I needed during the emotional roller coaster of the auditions. She never doubted that I'd make it to Hollywood and even go beyond.

As my eyes grew heavy, I closed my journal and drifted off to sleep. I slept well and woke at four to the sound of the alarm clock's buzzer.

For the next two hours I showered, vocalized, put on *way* too much makeup, and worked on curling every single hair on my head. If nothing else went right that day, at least from the neck up I would look perfect.

But you know what they say about the best-laid plans of mice and men. . . .

A Dismal Beginning

When Pam and I went downstairs, we discovered that the skies had opened in a torrential downpour. Since I didn't have an umbrella, every curl I had labored over drooped as we hurried from the taxi to the stadium where the auditions would be held. Though I was discouraged because of my ruined hair, I counted my blessings when we stopped by a restroom. Dozens of girls crowded the mirrors, all of them desperately trying to curl their hair, brush their teeth, and bathe in the sink. Unlike me, these women hadn't been fortunate enough to have a hotel room provided for them.

I repaired my hair as best I could and walked out, resolving never to complain again.

I couldn't believe how many people had descended on Chicago—almost fifteen thousand had come to Soldier Field to audition for a chance to be on the show. The *American Idol* staff had begun wristbanding and ticketing at six in the morning the day before, and they worked around the clock until eight in the morning on audition day. Again I thanked the Lord that Pam and I hadn't had to spend the night in the arena. Thousands did.

As we made our way to the special section reserved for contest winners, I reviewed a mental list of the things required for all entrants: two forms of identification, a release form, proof that we were between the ages of sixteen and twenty-eight as of August 15, 2005, and one prepared song to be sung without accompaniment of any kind. We'd been told that if we passed the first test, we might have to sing two more songs a cappella.

One would be a song of our choice; the other would be from a list provided by a producer.

When we first walked into the arena, I saw the special set of bleachers reserved for contest winners. Directly across from this section was an area filled with thousands of others who would be auditioning. These people weren't standing quietly, biding their time—they were performing for TV cameramen who wandered throughout the crowd, trailed by producers and others scouting around for interesting shots.

The energy level in that place was high enough to power a small city. No one whispered or held casual conversations; everybody was singing, talking, or yelling. One girl stood on a bench and sang at the top of her lungs, belting out a song as if she'd already moved into the finals.

I bit my lip and followed Pam through the crowd. Like the situation at the radio station, most of the people I met were friendly, but their smiles were tempered by a speculative curiosity about my potential for competition.

Every once in a while I'd hear a sudden buzz in the crowd and feel a shift, usually the result of a celebrity appearance. Ryan Seacrest, the blond, boyish host of *American Idol,* stepped out at one point, and so did Jennifer Hudson and George Huff, both finalists on *Idol*'s third season. I had watched the show since its beginning, and I gaped in delight as Jennifer and George walked past the bleachers.

They were two of my all-time favorite contestants. Though not as large as I am, Jennifer was representing for the big girls just as I hoped to. From the moment I saw her first audition in season three, I loved her powerful voice. I was amazed and disappointed when she was eliminated way too early.

George had a contagious joy that I just *knew* came from

the Lord. My suspicions were validated when he released his debut gospel CD, *Miracles.* I bought it the day it came out and loved it.

I nearly had to pinch myself at the thought of two "Idols" in my midst. They had walked the road I was hoping to travel myself.

I wondered if they loved the spotlight and the murmur that followed them everywhere they went. What was it like, knowing that people wanted to know everything about you?

I wanted to know where Jennifer shopped, where George went to church, and whether Simon was as mean as he appeared to be on television. I wanted to ask who had influenced them musically and whether they had ever met any of their musical idols.

Had either George or Jennifer met Oprah? I thought about what I would do if I ever came face-to-face with Oprah or with my childhood musical influence, Whitney Houston. If someone were to introduce us, I don't think I would be able to utter a single word to either woman.

I had so many questions I wished I could ask Jennifer and George. Above all, I wondered if I would make it as far as they had.

Into the Arena

We had arrived at Soldier Field at six, and we sat in a sheltered area inside the stadium for three hours before the producers began the auditions. I'll be honest, every moment you see on television looks exciting, but contestants do a lot of sitting and waiting during the audition phase.

At nine the staff began to move us from the indoor bleachers into the fourteen tents that had been set up on the field.

The rain had stopped, though the outside air was still damp with mist. A freezing wind blew off Lake Michigan, and I had to clench my jaw to keep my teeth from chattering.

Those of us who were fortunate enough to be contest winners were allowed to audition first. Each group of four of us was sent to a tent, where we would sing for one of the show's many assistant producers.

I found myself in the sixth group to move into a tent. Behind a table sat a black lady who looked to be in her early thirties. She looked like someone I might be friends with, so I felt a little less nervous—until she looked up. In a stern voice she told us that we would sing our prepared song and she would stop us when she'd heard enough.

With me were a plus-sized white girl (I confess I was happy not to be the only big contestant in the group), a young white guy, and another young girl, who looked to be of mixed race. My sister in the weight struggle sang a country song I had never heard before. *Not bad*, I thought.

The producer lifted her hand to indicate she'd heard enough. She told the girl to prepare her next song, then she looked at the young man standing next to me. He sang a stirring rendition of the Temptations' "I Heard It through the Grapevine," and I thought he was incredible. I didn't expect that deep, husky, soulful voice to come out of him.

I shouldn't have been surprised at how good the others were. We had, after all, already won regional contests, but that fact didn't seem to impress the producer behind the table. With an expressionless face she instructed him to prepare his next song as well. Then she glared at me as if to say, "What have *you* got?"

With all the performance skills I could muster, I let loose with my bouncy rendition of "Rock Steady." As I sang, I snapped my fingers, shook my generous hips, and looked the producer square in the eye. If I was going home, I was going home after giving it my all.

When I had finished, the producer said, "Step back, please."

What? No "prepare your next song" for me?

> If I was going home, I was going home after giving it my all.

I stepped back, but my thoughts were roiling. Maybe she simply forgot to tell me to prepare another song. Maybe she didn't need to hear anything else because I'd been really good—or really awful.

My mind raced as the last girl sang Alicia Keys's "If I Ain't Got You." I wasn't paying much attention until she let loose in the most amazing vocal run I had ever heard. That little girl could flat *sing*.

When the producer instructed her to prepare her second song, I felt the tang of disappointment. All three of my fellow contestants had been incredible, yet I was the only one who had not been told to get ready to sing again.

I was still hoping the producer had simply forgotten, so as the first girl began to sing her second song, I reviewed my second song, just in case. I was on my third run-through when the guy next to me bellowed out another soulful classic, then stepped back to wait.

I held my breath, then realized my preparation was all for nothing when the producer looked past me to the last girl. As the fourth girl sang Christina Aguilera's "Beautiful," my heart sank. I'd gotten up in the middle of the night, sat in the cramped and loud stadium for three hours, and dragged Pam all the way from Atlanta only to be eliminated in the *first round?* That lady must have really hated me.

Finally she leaned forward to announce her verdict.

She asked contestants one, two, and four to step forward, then gave them the smallest of smiles. "Thank you so much for coming here today. You all have really good voices and have the potential to go far . . . but I will not be passing you to the next round."

She continued to speak, but I didn't hear anything else because her first statement kept echoing in my brain. One, two, and four didn't make it. So, by process of elimination . . . I did.

I did?

Speechless, I turned around and looked for Pam, who stood at a discreet distance, trying to see what was happening. I gave her a thumbs-up sign, which spurred her to run around the bleachers shrieking, "I knew it! I knew it! Go, Roomdawg! That's my Roomdawg!"

Leaving Pam to run amok, I turned to face the producer. The woman gave me a warm smile, revealing a pair of matching dimples, and nodded at me. "You'll be moving on. 'Rock Steady' is a good song for you, but I think you need to work on your performance a little." Then she handed me a yellow sheet of paper.

I stared at it as if I'd never seen paper before. "What's this?"

"It'll get you into the second round," she said. "Go up the stairs to the Cadillac Club; that's where you'll wait for your audition with Ken and Nigel."

Ken Warwick and Nigel Lythgoe, I knew, were the executive producers of *American Idol.* (With Simon Fuller, Nigel also created *So You Think You Can Dance.*) In a way, the thought of singing for them was even more nerve-racking than singing for Paula, Randy, and Simon.

I stepped out of the tent and walked toward the Cadillac Club on legs that felt as quivery as Jell-O. Because they had set up barricades to keep family members from mingling with the contestants, I caught Pam's eye and yelled that I was on my way to sing for Nigel and Ken. My advancement meant we had to part for a while.

The Cadillac Club

Upstairs I had to wait in another line to have my picture taken and sign a number of documents. The atmosphere was a lot more pleasant than that of the field. Most of the people who came through the Cadillac Club doorway were happy and/or screaming because they couldn't believe they'd made it through the first round.

I'd heard that the first round was the toughest to survive. After watching four seasons of the show, I suspected that the producers sometimes allowed people to progress even if they weren't spectacular singers—in fact, some of them weren't gifted singers at all. I figured they did it because *American Idol* is a TV show first and a singing competition second.

If you've watched *American Idol* at all, especially footage of the early rounds, you've probably been amazed to hear some really bad singers insist that they're really good. Although it is true that what a singer hears in his or her ears is different from what a listener hears, there's another reason those people honestly believe they're viable contenders for the title of American Idol: Not only do their families and friends assure them that they're fantastic, but their advancement to the next level also confirms that belief.

As a result, they're often shocked when they stand before the three television judges and hear that they're not good. Their distress, disbelief, and dismay create dramatic moments—and spellbinding television.

(Since my *American Idol* experience, I view the beginning of the season a little differently. I have met several people who recognize me slightly but confess that they watch only the first few weeks of *Idol* because they love laughing at all the bad singers. I know. It can be entertaining. But I can't help but feel compassion for the countless numbers of hopefuls who leave feeling crushed because their hopes have been dashed into a million little pieces.)

After I showed my identification again and completed more paperwork, a producer gave me the lyrics to "Lady Marmalade," a song recorded by Labelle in 1975 and popularized again in the 2001 movie *Moulin Rouge*. Was I supposed to learn this song? Without any music?

No one seemed to have any answers. I took the lyrics sheet and moved into another room, where everyone in sight was busy practicing "Lady Marmalade." We had no score, so people who didn't know the song were trying to stand next to folks who did so they could pick up the melody. I set my sights on a young sista who looked vaguely familiar. She was belting it out and sounded as if she knew the song backward and forward, so I figured she'd be a reliable teacher.

Have you ever walked into a band room where every instrumentalist is warming up? That's about what this rehearsal room sounded like. Everyone sang in different keys and practiced different lines. If we hadn't been so nervous, the situation might have been comical.

I learned that my "Lady Marmalade" tutor had made it to the Hollywood round in *Idol's* season three. When we had a chance to talk, she told us that during the Hollywood group round, she and two others had partnered with a girl who refused to work. As a result, the judges eliminated her entire group.

That's when I remembered her. The producers highlighted her group that year because the situation added great drama. She was an incredible singer. With her powerful voice, slender frame, and pretty face, she had the American Idol "look." I felt certain she would make it to Hollywood this season, too.

To soothe the singers' throats, the caterers had furnished a table with hot tea, lemon, and honey. I made myself a cup of tea and sipped it as I studied the lyrics sheet.

I was wearing a top with a sheer layer of black chiffon, and the numbers they'd given us wouldn't stick to my blouse. I peeled off my number—6369—and held it with my lyrics, figuring I'd just hold it up as I sang.

By this time it was nearly noon, and the practice room had filled up with about a hundred people. We hadn't heard a word about lunch, but I was too tense to think about food. Everyone else must have felt the same way.

Finally, someone came in and began to organize us into groups of ten. I joined a group of nine others and followed a producer into a conference room. "You'll have to be ready with one fast song and one slow song," the *Idol* staffer told us. "We're only going to ask for 'Lady Marmalade' from a few people, so don't worry too much about it. That song won't have any bearing on whether or not you make it to the next round." I was relieved to hear my success wouldn't depend on "Lady Marmalade," but I wished I had known earlier so I could have worked on the songs I would actually have to sing.

I stood fourth in line in my ten-person group, and the first two people who went to sing for the producers came out of the room crying because they didn't make it. Third in line was my

"Lady Marmalade" tutor. When she came out with a downcast face, I felt hopeless. The cameraman captured her every emotion as she told the camera, "They said to work on my vibrato."

If they thought her *vibrato was bad,* I thought, *they are sure to hate me. Mine is out of control!*

When I walked into the audition room, I saw Ken and Nigel seated at a table, with a crew working in the shadows behind them. As cameras rolled and my heart pounded, I smiled and tried to act as if I were the most confident performer in Chicago.

I told them my name and age and said I was from Tennessee. When I said I wanted to sing "Rock Steady," Ken acted as if he didn't know the tune.

I sang a little of the song, but Ken stopped me and asked if I could sing something more current. The question caught me off guard—more *current?* I figured the Jackson 5's version of "Who's Lovin' You" wouldn't qualify. For a moment my mind went blank; then I began to mentally sift through all the songs in my iTunes collection.

> I sang two lines before they cut me off with an abrupt thank-you.

Nigel spoke up while I was sifting. "Do you know any Janet Jackson or Alicia Keys?"

I nodded. "I can do 'Fallin'.'"

"Good."

I sang two lines before they cut me off with an abrupt thank-you.

I felt as if I stood on the edge of a crumbling cliff when Ken turned to Nigel and spoke as if I weren't even in the room: "Yeah, she's good. But she has that gospel diva thing that gets so boring after a while because we see so much of it."

My heart sank.

He continued talking to Nigel. "What do *you* think?"

Nigel looked at me. "Oh, it's a definite *yes* for me."

My eyes must have bulged out of my head. I felt as if Ken hated me but Nigel loved me. What were they going to do—split me down the middle?

"Am I in?" I didn't mean to ask the question aloud, but the words slipped out before I could stop them.

"Congratulations," Nigel announced. My screams nearly drowned out Ken's muttering about singing more contemporary songs. I hurried out of the room, grabbing a yellow ticket on the way—the one thing I needed in order to stand before Paula, Simon, and Randy.

As soon as I moved through the doorway, cameras zoomed in on my face. I was so happy that I was crying, yet I felt a strange pressure to perform for the camera.

Someone kept asking, "How do you feel?" and all I could do was answer, "I feel great."

Someone asked if I had anyone I could call. Yes! I tried to call Pam and couldn't reach her. The cameras followed as I walked away. The interviewer kept asking what I was going to say to Paula, Randy, and Simon, but I didn't have a clue. I kept thinking that I'd be singing for that trio later in the day; then one of the *Idol* staffers told me I wouldn't sing for the television judges until four days later.

I couldn't believe it. I had to stay in Chicago and wait *four more days?* Star 94 had agreed to pay for one night at my hotel. To top it all off, my friend Chance was getting married that weekend, and Chance and Jennifer's wedding was going to be the social event of the year. I had been looking forward to it for so long. How could I miss *that?*

I didn't know what to do. Should I fly home and come back? Would it be better to stay in Chicago? Paying for a week in a luxury hotel would be painfully expensive, but flying back and forth would drain my bank account too.

When I finally caught up with Pam, she hugged me so hard she nearly choked me. "You made it, and look at all the people who didn't," she screamed. In retrospect, that might not have been the best thing to shout in front of all the disappointed people leaving the auditions. I felt the sting of more than a few narrowed glances shot in my direction—obviously, some people were wondering what I had that they didn't.

I didn't blame them. I kept wondering the same thing.

Supporting Others' Gifts

To this day, I am uncomfortable in that kind of cutthroat, competitive environment. I've spent a lot of time around Christian singers, and they are usually supportive and appreciative of someone else's gift. Most Christian artists recognize each others' differing abilities and rejoice in them because we all fill a different role in the body of Christ.

Scripture demonstrates that there is room for *many* musicians in the Lord's service. When King David was planning the Temple in Israel, he stipulated that the worship team should consist of four *thousand* musicians (see 1 Chronicles 23:5). Certain families were even set apart for music making in the Lord's service: "All these men were under the direction of their fathers as they made music at the house of the LORD. Their responsibilities included the playing of cymbals, harps, and lyres at the house of God. Asaph, Jeduthun, and Heman reported directly to the king. They and their families were all trained in making music before the LORD, and each of them—288 in all—was an accomplished musician. The musicians were appointed to their term of service by means of sacred lots, without regard to whether they were young or old, teacher or student" (1 Chronicles 25:6-8).

My life experience was rich with memories and examples of talented people who set their egos aside in order to worship the One who blesses us with life. Though we strove to present an excellent musical offering, we didn't judge one another. We knew that God can use anything to praise Him or carry His message, even folks who are doing well to make a joyful noise.

But I didn't see many examples of mutual support at the *Idol* auditions in Chicago. I did meet a few believers in the crowd, people who were encouraging and kind, but I also encountered a lot of cutting competitiveness.

When our work was done for the day, Pam and I went shopping. I knew I had to learn some more contemporary songs, and since I don't regularly listen to pop radio, I didn't know what songs would be suitable. I went into a couple of record stores and asked what was popular so I could begin to pick up some new tunes.

I also addressed my problem of what to do about the next round of auditions—the round that would decide whether or not I would go with the other *Idol* contestants to Hollywood. After speaking with Chance and hearing him give me his blessing to miss the wedding, I called some friends and family to see if any of them knew anyone in Chicago. My best friend, Chandra, had a cousin near the city, and Alberta and her family were kind enough to take me in. I didn't have a week's worth of clothes with me, so I spent most of those four days practicing, praying, and doing laundry.

As I prayed, once again I found myself asking God what He

was up to. I hadn't expected to make it that far, and I wondered what He was planning. Had He brought me to this *Idol* experience because He wanted me to reach a certain destination, or was this more about lessons I'd learn on the journey? Since a godly woman's steps are ordered by the Lord, I knew I was traveling on the road God had ordained for me. But my flashlight of faith illuminated only a few feet of the path ahead.

Hearing God

One day, Joetta McGhee, a friend from California, called me. After we made small talk for a while, she told me she'd called because she wanted to talk about something "pretty deep."

I settled myself comfortably on the couch and prepared for a good heart-to-heart.

Joetta got right to her question: "How do you hear from God?"

She explained that she was unhappy at her job and felt God had something else in store for her, but she didn't know how to know what it was. She remembered that I'd waited for the Lord's guidance after graduation and had ended up working at LifeWay. She recalled that I had turned down other positions because I felt I'd heard from God about where I was to work.

"So," she asked, "how did you know?"

Wouldn't it be nice if there were some formula we could apply so we could hear from God anytime we needed to know His will? Or what if God spoke in an audible voice every time He wanted to get our attention? Now *that* would be hard to miss!

Yet if we relied on a step-by-step process or on the certainty that we would hear him speak (in a voice that simply *must* sound like James Earl Jones), would we be willing to wait for Him to make His will clear? Would we enjoy seeking Him and spending time with Him? Or would we simply go through the motions and expect Him always to be at our beck and call?

Rest assured, God knows us better than we know ourselves. He *does* speak to His children—in His time and in His way.

Since I had enjoyed such sweet times with the Lord the first time I worked through the *Experiencing God* Bible study, I decided to do the study again. In the workbook that accompanies the study, author Henry Blackaby lists seven realities of experiencing God. The fourth reality is this: "God speaks by the Holy Spirit through the Bible, prayer, circumstances, and the church to reveal Himself, His purposes, and His ways."[1] I have found that statement to be absolutely true.

I explained to Joetta that while I've never heard God speak in an audible voice, He usually makes Himself very clear. He often speaks after I've spent concentrated time in prayer and seeking to know His will. I sometimes hear His voice in the form of an idea or an impression.

Often God speaks to me through other people. I told Joetta about the times people kept asking me to lead worship at their churches. Even though I protested that I was not a worship leader, they disagreed and continued to ask. That was God speaking.

I also reminded Joetta about the time God spoke to me through the LifeWay logo on the back of my workbook—in that case, God communicated through my circumstances.

Every time I open the Bible, God speaks to me. The Bible is God's written Word; often I hear Him address my specific situation through the Scriptures. Whatever channel God uses, when I hear His voice, I recognize it, and I act accordingly.

Now, in Chicago, as I waited for my audition before the judges, I sat on the couch or stood by the washing machine during my prayer time, and the Lord assured me that He was with me.

Then I heard the quiet inner voice that I've come to recognize through time spent with God and in His Word promise that I would make it further than I had anticipated.

I shivered in excitement as I considered what lay ahead.

Here Come the Judges

Before I could sing for the three television judges, I had to report to the W Hotel for an extensive interview. There I spoke with an *Idol* staffer who wanted to know about my background, my job, where I came from—pretty much my life story. I learned that of the 15,000 people who auditioned for *Idol* in Chicago, only 250 had made it to this round. Paula, Randy, and Simon would hear 125 of us on the first day, 125 on the second.

A couple of days later, I went back to the W Hotel to sing for the television judges. We all lined up and waited outside the hotel, and the sight of so many hopefuls on the street was really comical. We had been instructed to wear the same outfit we'd worn for the first audition. Some people had dressed in outlandish costumes on that first day, hoping to catch a producer's eye.

Those crazy outfits appeared again, worn by contestants now hoping to catch the TV judges' attention. About thirty people stood in the line in front of me, including one hairy-legged guy dressed like Dorothy from *The Wizard of Oz*. Another guy wore a hula skirt and a snug Chicago Bears football jersey. One man had dressed like the Statue of Liberty; a lady came to the audition in roller skates; and a young girl wearing a prom dress kept proclaiming that she was going to ask Ryan Seacrest to the prom!

I was back in my black blouse with the chiffon overlayer—

not the warmest outfit in the world. Again the cold lake wind bit at us; most of the people took turns asking others to hold their place in line while they ran down to a nearby McDonald's for an Egg McMuffin and coffee.

I wasn't nearly as nervous this time around. I hadn't expected to get this far, and for some reason the thought of standing before Paula, Simon, and Randy didn't frighten me. I was wary of Simon, of course—you'd have to live in a cave to be unaware of his acerbic tongue—but I'd seen those three in my living room so many times that I couldn't help feeling as if I were about to sing for old friends.

Wearing my assigned number, I followed the others into a large room, where we were seated. I could tell that the producers were seating us strategically. Though I couldn't determine who was going to make it and who wasn't, it seemed to me that the weaker singers were spread throughout the crowd. Only contestants were allowed into this room, so all family members and friends had to wait outside.

Once again, we had nothing to do but wait.

When I'm alone, I like to spend time getting focused and enter what I call "the zone," but I couldn't help noticing that while we waited, the producers had assigned cameramen to record interviews with certain contestants. They spent a lot of time with Lauren, a Puerto Rican girl sitting near me. After listening to her interview, I was extremely impressed with Lauren's story and her eloquence. After a necessary surgery on her vocal chords,

> The thought of standing before Paula, Simon, and Randy didn't frighten me—I'd seen those three in my living room so many times I couldn't help feeling as if I were about to sing for old friends.

her doctor had told her she might never be able to sing again. She told the interviewer that her presence at the *auditions* was a miracle and, win or lose, knowing that she'd experienced a taste of the miraculous was enough for her.

Another producer turned his attention to identical twins Derrell and Terrell Brittenum. Those guys were characters! As an *American Idol* aficionado, I knew that several sets of twins audition each season. They usually dress alike and play up their "twin status" to advance to the next round. In the past, however, few of the singing twins had been vocally strong enough to get to Hollywood.

I had heard the Brittenums singing outside and felt certain they would make it to California. Not only were they great singers, but the charismatic young men also looked great on TV.

In front of me the producers zoomed in on a girl wearing fishnet stockings, Gina Glocksen. She had auditioned last season and had made it to this point but not to Hollywood. When I saw how the producers singled Gina out, I became convinced that this would be her year for advancement, not mine. No one came over to interview me.

Not a good sign.

Rockin' Steady

After four hours they finally called my row to approach the judges' room. We sat in chairs placed along the wall in the hallway outside the room, so I sat between Gina and a guy who kept singing along with the music from his Walkman. I could tell he didn't have a superstrong voice, so I assumed he and I would be cut in this round.

As I waited, I remembered hearing what the Lord had impressed on me in my prayer time. He had said I would go further than I expected, but I didn't have the courage to trust that promise for the future. I had *already* gone further than I expected, so I was more than willing to "let the Lord off the hook."

It might also have been that the little girl in me was afraid to risk anything else; I don't know. But I do know I braced myself for disappointment while I sat in that chair.

Just before it was our group's turn to go in, the judges took a lunch break, leaving us with another hour and a half to kill. Simon and Paula passed by us on their way to lunch, and Paula greeted us and said we could go get something to eat.

Some of the contestants did, but I had decided to fast that day. I always felt closer to the Lord when I fasted, so on the plane ride to Chicago I decided to fast before as many auditions as the Lord allowed me. I wanted to be in the center of God's will, so I stayed in my chair and prayed quietly, asking the Lord to bless me with favor and beauty. If I was going to be disappointed in another couple of hours, I wanted to be surrounded by the Lord's comfort on the way out the door.

The guy next to me didn't go to lunch either. Oblivious to the fact that I was praying, he kept singing two different songs and asking my opinion about his selections. I wanted to be honest, but I didn't want to hurt his feelings. I told him that either song worked just fine. As I smiled at him, I noticed armpit stains on his T-shirt and wondered if he'd spent his four days of waiting sleeping on the street somewhere.

Finally lunch ended, and we were on deck. As Gina stood and walked into the judges' room, I caught Ryan Seacrest's attention and told him—truthfully—that I brought greetings from Steve and Vikki at Star 94 in Atlanta, where Ryan had worked when he lived in Georgia. I called out to him with a lot more bravado than I felt, but Ryan stopped to talk to me, which was probably a good thing. In any case, I felt more confident when Gina came out screaming that she'd made it to the next round. Summoning my courage, I left her with Ryan and strolled into the judges' room.

When I saw Paula, Randy, and Simon sitting behind a table, I forced a smile. "Now I know you just put someone else through," I told them, with what I hoped was a saucy air, "but you're about to do the same thing right now."

They all chuckled, and Randy asked my name. When I replied, "Mandisa," Randy asked, "Mandisa what?" Because my unusual name has been mangled for years—I've often been called Mandy Sahundley—I made a snap decision. One name was enough to deal with on national television.

> Because my unusual name has been mangled for years, I made a snap decision. One name was enough to deal with on national television.

"Just Mandisa," I said; then I added that I was a session singer and a worship leader.

Simon informed me that all the session singers he knows don't really *want* to be session singers, implying, of course, that what they really want to be is a star.

I tried to convince him that I really enjoyed my job, but I could tell he was trying to trap me into saying something more controversial when he continued to toss questions my way. "Do you think you are better than the people you do sessions with?" he asked.

Struggling to maintain a balance between humility and confidence, I told him I thought I was meant to do more than sing backup for the rest of my life.

"Well." Randy crossed his arms. "Since you're a session

singer, you can sing on pitch and maintain a good tone. You're really gonna bring it, right?"

I smiled and nodded. "Watch this."

And then, with courage I didn't know I possessed, I sang "Rock Steady" and even remembered to snap my fingers and move as if I were having the time of my life. Paula clapped along, and Randy danced in his chair.

When I'd finished, Randy commented that after all my talk of being a session singer, he hadn't been disappointed. Simon said I was "really, really good. You have a great voice and a pretty face. Everything I'd hoped you'd be, you were on that."

"You definitely have the pipes," Paula added. "You even had Simon dancing in his seat."

Then, together, they looked at each other and counted: "One, two, three—you're going to Hollywood!"

I went out the door screaming, overjoyed with the result and with their comments. More than anything, I was grateful and amazed that Simon had said I had a pretty face—after I'd been so terrified he'd say something about my weight!

Ryan Seacrest came over with a camera crew and asked how I felt. "This feels like heaven!" I told him.

I'm sure how I felt can't hold a candle to heaven, but that moment was the most heavenly I'd known in my lifetime. I practically floated to the next desk, where an *Idol* staffer told me I couldn't tell anybody except my parents that I'd made it to the Hollywood round. I'd have to keep everything secret until the show aired in January. Four months of enforced silence!

More than anything, I was grateful and amazed that Simon had said I had a pretty face—after I'd been so terrified he'd say something about my weight!

Let me tell you, it wasn't easy.

Despite my happiness, a few disturbing questions hovered around the edges of my mind. In order to maintain confidentiality, I was told that I needed to shut down my Web site. This presented a problem, because people who wanted to invite me to lead worship or to sing usually contacted me through my Web site. How was I supposed to earn a living while I waited to see if anything would come out of this *Idol* experience?

I had also nearly completed my first solo CD, a collection of songs I planned to offer for sale. People who heard me sing at churches were always asking how they could purchase my music, so I used my own funds to finance a low-budget recording. I had announced an October release date to those on my mailing list, but the *Idol* producers told me I wouldn't be able to sell it.

How could I explain the CD's unavailability without mentioning *American Idol*—or being deceptive?

I couldn't see any answers, but I knew the Lord was bigger than any problem looming on the horizon. I'd trusted Him so far, so I'd keep trusting Him on the path that led to Hollywood—and whatever complications it might bring.

4 The Joy of Trusting

On December second I joined Beth Moore's worship team for an event in Fresno, California. Because I was to fly to Los Angeles for the next round of *Idol* competition after we finished the event, my emotions were spinning like food in a blender.

I loved singing with Travis Cottrell and the worship team. I admire Beth Moore tremendously and believe she is an anointed and extremely effective Bible teacher. I have learned so much about the Lord as a result of sitting under her teaching.

When I'm leading worship with her team, moments fly by as I enjoy what is almost like an out-of-body experience. I purposely try to lose myself when I'm worshipping and singing to the Lord. I don't focus on hitting high notes or demonstrating showmanship; I focus on honoring Jesus. He's more impressed with a receptive heart than a trained voice.

This particular event in Fresno was special for several reasons. First, it served as a bit of a "send-off" for me. I had been faithful to recite that line about the confidentiality agreement to anyone who asked about the Chicago auditions. But unlike the other forty Beth Moore events in which I'd participated, I wasn't going home Saturday afternoon with the rest of the team—I was jetting off to Hollywood for mysterious reasons I couldn't explain.

Travis and the rest of the team realized what was up, and I knew they'd be praying for me.

In addition to being my send-off, the Fresno event was special because it was close enough to Sacramento for my mother to attend. Mom had become a familiar face at the Living Proof Live events. She had been to several, especially since making a commitment to follow Jesus at an event in November 2001. My heart always warmed when I looked into the audience and saw Mom with her hands raised and her eyes brimming with tears as she gazed toward the Father in worship.

Last, the Fresno event was special because the Lord spoke extraordinarily through Beth that weekend. She used Psalm 40 to exhort us to abandon ourselves to the mystery of God.

The Psalmist's Pit of Despair

Several of those verses rang with particular resonance within my heart:

> *I waited patiently for the LORD to help me,*
> *and he turned to me and heard my cry.*
> *He lifted me out of the pit of despair,*
> *out of the mud and the mire.*
> *He set my feet on solid ground*
> *and steadied me as I walked along.*

He has given me a new song to sing,
  a hymn of praise to our God.
Many will see what he has done and be amazed.
  They will put their trust in the LORD.

PSALM 40:1-3

David's psalm echoed my own prayer: No matter what happened in California, I wanted people to know that my life revolves around and is dependent on God. He took me, a drifting and uncertain girl, and set me on solid ground. I wanted to be a singer, but I wanted to be *His* singer.

> No matter what happened in California, I wanted people to know that my life revolves around and is dependent upon God.

On Saturday morning, to begin our final day together, Beth and the praise team gathered to prepare ourselves for the final sessions of the conference. Anyone who peered in at us would have said we were huddled in a regular old locker room at the Selland Arena, but to us the space was a sanctuary, and we were about to call down fire from heaven.

The ghosts of sweaty socks and wet towels had been eradicated by the sweet scent of a vanilla-and-brown-sugar candle. A table, draped in green cloth, held bread and grape juice from the Communion service we'd held the night before. My friend Tammy Jensen and I sat on a bench and tingled with excitement for what we were about to hear. Friday night's session had been powerful, and Beth had ended with a teaser about what was to come this morning. She would continue teaching from the fortieth psalm, focusing on the anatomy of the pit.

In Beth's testimony she is always very clear about how the

Lord rescued her from abuse and destruction. I think that is why I've always felt a connection to her. God pulled her out of a pit, and He was in the process of doing the same thing for me, a woman in the grip of food addiction.

As we team members positioned ourselves to beg the Lord for His blessing, an inexplicable feeling of sorrow came over me. We began to pray, and my thoughts drifted back to my first event with this team, four and a half years earlier in Charlotte. Even as the new kid on the block I had felt instant camaraderie with these people.

The well of memory opened, and a flood of bittersweet nostalgia overwhelmed me. I recalled the many times I had knelt as we prayed before each event. I often began our prayer time upright, but by the time the final amen had been said, I would be prostrate on the floor, overwhelmed by the presence of God.

On that night in Fresno, I felt humbled and honored that God had placed me in this position of service to the body of Christ. As I flashed back to the laughs and tears our worship team had shared, the love of God warmed my soul. Like a teapot boiling over, my emotions spilled out in a stream of tears that rolled down my freshly made-up face.

Before I could even reach for a tissue, Beth, Travis, Tammy, Chance, and the other team members encircled me and laid their hands on my head, shoulders, and arms as they prayed for me. They asked God to send me out in His power and surround me with His angels. Beth asked that my voice would flow out of me in a way it never had before, that the sound would shock even me. They concluded by asking the Lord to protect me, use me, and bless me with His favor.

As the room rang out with amens, I felt as if my spirit had caught fire. I was ready for *anything*.

We walked out of our prayer room to face seven thousand Christian women, all of whom were ready to receive a blessing and wisdom from God. We leaped onto the stage with the joy of the Lord as the source of our enthusiasm. I worshipped as if this would be my last chance to sing before seeing Jesus face-to-face.

With every song we sang, I became more convinced that this would be my last event. I was still unsure about how far I would make it on the *American Idol* journey, but I sang with my sisters in Christ and gave everything to the Lord.

As the event came to an end, Travis signaled our guitar player, Kevin, to begin the intro to "Shackles." We had already sung the song three times, so I was surprised Travis would call for it again.

The Mary Mary song "Shackles (Praise You)" has long been a favorite of mine because it speaks so clearly to my heart and mind. The lyrics talk about how we often have difficulty believing that God is bigger than our struggles, but He is! The songwriter says God has the power to remove the shackles from our feet so that we can dance and praise Him.

The lyrics don't specify any particular struggle, but the thing that has always kept me shackled is my habit of overeating. Not all food addictions are obvious—many anorexics and bulimics are able to disguise their destructive habits with clothing or carefully cultivated rituals—but nothing screams "overeater" like a plus-sized body.

Not all food addictions are obvious—but nothing screams "overeater" like a plus-sized body.

I had recorded "Shackles" for one of Travis's CDs back when I was still working in customer service at LifeWay. Ever since that recording session I have felt the song was my testimony set to music. I could sing that song like no other because the words poured straight out of my soul.

In Fresno, when I felt the other worship singers physically surround me as I concluded the first verse, I knew I was headed for an emotional breakdown.

Just get me through the song, I prayed. But sometimes the Lord wants us to display our emotions because they assure us we're human . . . and vulnerable.

Somehow I kept it together through the second verse:

> *Everything that could go wrong*
> *All went wrong at one time*
> *So much pressure fell on me*
> *I thought I was gon' lose my mind*
> *But I know You wanna see*
> *If I will hold on through these trials,*
> *But I need You to lift this load,*
> *'Cause I can't take it no more.*

As I felt those dear and familiar hands rubbing my back, I lost it. For the second time that day, tears streamed down my cheeks as I tried to sing through the bridge:

> *Been through the fire and the rain*
> *Bound in every kind of way*
>
> *But God has broken every chain*
> *So let me go right now.*

By the time I got to the final chorus, I had to drop my microphone to my side so I could release a sob. I stood there on the stage and had an "ugly cry"—the sort where your nose crinkles and your mouth twists into an unnatural grimace. I sobbed and hoped no one was capturing this moment on videotape.

And that poor audience! They must have wondered what in the world was wrong with me. There was no way they could know I wasn't caught up in guilt or grief; I was saying good-bye to my family, a family in which I had never known anything but concern, acceptance, and unconditional love.

I came away from the Fresno event believing that the greatest thrill of my life would be knowing God deeper and better each day. Living hand in hand with Him would be the wildest ride anyone could ever hope for!

One Chapter Ends, Another Begins

With my head still feeling swollen from tears, the day after the Fresno event I boarded a plane and flew to Los Angeles for the next round of the *Idol* competition. During the hiatus between Chicago and the Hollywood round, the *Idol* staff conducted background checks on all qualifying contestants. Of the 175 people who made it to the next round, only 165 actually got to compete in Hollywood.

After we arrived, we waited around for a while—surprise!—and finally checked into our hotel. Then the show staffers called us into a meeting.

As I looked at the other contestants, I thought I'd wandered into a production of *America's Next Top Model* by mistake. The gorgeous girls around me were all wearing short skirts and halter tops, and they all had slammin' hair and flawless makeup. I stood against the wall, too intimidated to wander into the group and make conversation.

> As I looked at the other contestants, I thought I'd wandered into a production of *America's Next Top Model* by mistake.

The producers asked us to sit down. I was startled when who I thought was the Verizon "Can you hear me now?" guy took the microphone, but then I learned that the man before us wasn't the Verizon spokesman but Patrick Lynn, one of the head producers. He called us to order and explained that the next seven days would be the hardest week of our lives. He grinned, and I could feel the tension level rise in the room.

Patrick seemed to enjoy making us squirm. He bluntly told us that he wasn't there to make friends. "In fact," he added, "you'll probably hate me by the end of the week."

The people around me groaned, but I saw traces of humor in Patrick's eyes and smile. He had a quirky grin that lit his face every now and then, so even though he tried to be a hardnose, I liked him.

Patrick continued to explain that we'd be surrounded by cameras all week, so we needed to expect the unexpected. The producers wanted us to sing, but they also wanted stories that would make *Idol* a good TV show.

Tomorrow, he said, we would be divided into two groups. One group would go to the auditions while the other went on an excursion bus to tour Los Angeles. We would not learn which group we were in until we all met for breakfast.

With uncertainty hovering over our heads, we adjourned. Most of the contestants congregated in the hotel restaurant or gathered with friends to celebrate their accomplishment and size up their competition. But I was on a mission.

Before leaving Nashville for Fresno, I had felt the Lord directing me to write a series of devotionals for this audition week. So I wrote a separate lesson for each day, jotting down thoughts and Scripture verses focused on a variety of topics. As I completed my project, I felt the Lord telling me that this devotional would be not only for my use but also for three other people He would show me once I got to Hollywood.

I printed out three copies of each devotional booklet and put each manuscript into a gift bag along with a pocket Bible, Airborne (a product supposed to strengthen one's ability to fight colds), earplugs, and a sleep mask. I called these packages *American Idol* Survival Kits, and I asked the Lord to show me who was supposed to receive each bag.

I delivered the first bag to Karees, a girl I had met in the airport. I caught her off guard with my gift, but she thanked me over and over again. She then told me that she had auditioned last year and made it to Hollywood but was cut on the first day.

The possibility that I could be going home within a matter of hours unnerved me a little. I had already unpacked and ironed my clothes for the entire week. I'd be upset if I had done all that ironing for nothing—I *hate* ironing.

I felt led to give the second gift bag to a girl I'd not met before. I'd heard through the grapevine that Detrayshia had won a Christian singers' contest a few years back. When I went to deliver her bag, I met her roommate—Lauren from Chicago, the miracle girl! She welcomed me into her room and explained that Detrayshia wasn't there, but I could leave the bag and she would make sure Detrayshia got it.

I felt an instant connection with Lauren and wished I had another bag to give her, but since I had already written specific names inside the pocket Bibles, I moved on to my next recipient.

I had also met Rose, a twenty-one-year-old with beautiful eyes and a hilarious sense of humor, in the airport. She was with her mom and aunt in her room when I knocked on the door, and she began to cry when I gave her the bag.

When I asked if something was wrong, Rose explained that she was having a hard time with some of the negative personalities she'd encountered at the meeting. But my gift had reminded her that God cared for her and was with her, even in this hypercompetitive situation. I prayed with her and left the room convinced that I'd delivered the gift bags to the people the Lord had in mind.

Feeling like an agent of God's love, I returned to my room and got ready for bed. My roommate, Shelby, finally arrived and shared her wild adventure with me. She had come from Denver but was late because she'd missed her flight. To make matters worse, she was sick, so she wanted to get to bed right away.

I said a silent prayer for her and set my alarm clock for five.

First Day in Hollywood

The next morning, as we contestants gathered to find out our destination for the day, I learned that I would be going on the excursion along with Karees and Detrayshia. Shelby and Rose would be auditioning.

Before we split up, Rose came over to thank me for the devotional. In the first lesson, I'd written about faith and about trusting that God had a plan for your life. She said the message meant a lot to her and had given her everything she needed to face the day—in fact, she had shared it with another girl, who later came up to me and expressed her gratitude and amazement that I would do something so selfless.

Later I learned that Rose was eliminated that day, but I trust she hasn't forgotten that God has a definite plan for her life.

While Rose, Shelby, and half of the group prepared to audition, I went downstairs and climbed onto one of two double-decker buses. Because I'm an introvert and tend to be reserved when surrounded by forceful personalities, I spent most of the day gaping at the antics of some of the other contestants. Mugging for the cameras, they scampered to the top deck of the bus and braved the cold wind to shout greetings to people on the sidewalk—the surest way I know to lose your voice.

We did all the typical tourist things in L.A. We went to Grauman's Chinese Theater, walked to the corner of Hollywood and Vine, ran out to the water at the beach, and stopped at the Hollywood Bowl. The cameramen continually threaded their way through our group, getting shots of what they call "B roll"— footage they can use for human interest stories to round out the show. Most of what they were recording was silly shenanigans, but I knew I'd seen this sort of thing before on the show.

At the Hollywood Bowl, all the contestants went up on the stage and started singing in small groups. I stood back and watched as people showboated and strutted their stuff—it looked as if some of them were trying to intimidate the others, and the experience made me uncomfortable.

Derrell and Terrell Brittenum were one of two sets of twins who made it to Hollywood. In the middle of all the showboating, Terrell called out, "The next person to sing will be Mandisa."

Oh, no. The others turned, urging me on, but I ran like Forrest Gump, not willing to sing no matter how much they begged. I wasn't being coy; I really wasn't comfortable in that atmosphere.

After I'd made my escape, a girl named Veronica came up and cocked a brow. "You know," she said, "now you have everybody wondering what you sound like."

I tried to explain that I was shy in situations like that, but I don't think she believed me.

When I got back to the hotel, I discovered that my room-mate had been eliminated. Shelby packed her things, slept a few hours, and got up the next morning to discover she had only two hours to catch her ride to the airport for an early flight.

I dressed carefully, knowing that those who'd survived yesterday's audition were preparing for the bus tour of Los Angeles. I chose a flowing turquoise blouse and black pants and put my hair up in a clip. The hair clip was part of my strategy—I knew I had to do something to make the judges remember me.

Once again we went to the theater and sat around, as nervous as cats in a roomful of rocking chairs. While we waited, producers conducted interviews out in the vestibule. After someone called my name for my pre-audition interview, I walked out of the theater and found Ryan Seacrest conversing with a cameraman. He wasn't conducting the interviews, but I asked him if he would do mine.

He peered more closely at me. "How are you feeling today?" he asked. "You doin' okay?"

With the camera rolling, I said I was worried because my jaw was hurting a little bit. I had a bad case of dog jaw.

He frowned. "What's dog jaw?"

I pointed to a spot in the middle of my cheek. "Feel right there."

The instant he pressed his finger to my cheek, I leaned toward him and barked like a pit bull.

The cameraman and I laughed. When Ryan had recovered from the shock, he called for Simon Lythgoe, one of the producers, to come over. "Hey, Simon," he called, "Mandisa's got this condition called dog jaw."

Sipping from a cup of coffee, Simon walked toward us. His eyes filled with concern. "Dog jaw? What's that?"

I leaned toward him and pointed to my cheek. "Feel right there."

This time when I barked, Simon's coffee went flying. Ryan and I had a good laugh, and that little joke made it onto the show later in the season.

Finally it was my turn to sing for Paula, Simon, and Randy again. For this round, we'd all been sent a CD of twelve songs. Unlike the last round, when we sang a cappella, this time we would sing with a piano and background vocals.

When we first arrived at the theater, we were introduced to Michael Orland, the pianist, and Debra Byrd, the vocal coach, who goes by the name "Byrd." They called us up in groups according to our song choice. We could sing in any key, and we were allowed to work with the pianist to choose the proper range. We were also given an opportunity to work with Byrd, who listened to our selections and made a few comments on our approach.

When it came time to sing for the judges, we went in row by row, but no one announced any results until the entire row of contestants had been through the process.

Before we began to sing, we were supposed to state our names, ages, hometowns, and why we thought we should be the next American Idol. I looked at the three judges, smiled, and said, "My

"My name is Mandisa, I'm twenty-nine years old, and I feel I should be the next American Idol because you've had big guys in the past. Ruben represented you really well, but now it's time for a fabulous and thick sista to represent it for the big girls, and I'm the one."

name is Mandisa, I'm twenty-nine years old, and I feel I should be the next American Idol because you've had big guys in the past. Ruben represented you really well, but now it's time for a fabulous and thick sista to represent it for the big girls, and I'm the one."

Everybody in the audience of waiting contestants went crazy, clapping and cheering, and Randy laughed. The tune I'd chosen, Donna Summer's "Dim All the Lights," started out slow, but when the disco beat kicked in, I took the clip out of my hair, shook my mane free, and danced around the stage while I sang my heart out. Strategy—soon I'd see whether or not it had worked.

I got what every singer dreams of: a reaction of people screaming and cheering. I couldn't have asked for a better response from the audience. As the applause died down, I left the stage and waited for the rest of my row to finish . . . and for my heart to stop pounding.

Finally they called everyone in my row, including Karees and Detrayshia, back into the auditorium. We lined up while Paula called out numbers and asked people to step forward.

I was asked to step forward, so I felt hopeful, but you never know with reality television—they might have been singling out the ones who were going home. But when the last number had been called, Randy said, "Congratulations—front line, you're going on to the next round. Back line, you're going home."

Unfortunately, my friends Karees and Detrayshia stood in the back line.

During the exit interview, when the producers asked how I felt, I said I felt wonderful but didn't understand how great singers like Karees and Detrayshia didn't make it through.

I was excited to be progressing in the competition, but my

joy was tempered by the thought of my girls going home. I embraced Karees and Detrayshia and hoped they could feel my love for them.

One of the best things about *American Idol* was the opportunity to meet new challenges. One of the hardest was saying good-bye to new friends.

One of the best things about *American Idol* was the opportunity to meet new challenges. One of the hardest was saying good-bye to new friends.

We Are Reziliance!

When all the auditions had been completed, the producers brought the successful contestants from the first day into the auditorium and explained that we should immediately start to work on our group songs. I glanced at my watch—it was nearly midnight, and we'd been up since five that morning. But this was a competition, and they wanted to test the limits of our abilities.

The producers presented us with a new challenge: We had to choose one of five preselected songs, arrange ourselves into three- or four-person groups, and start choreographing our dance moves and harmonies.

Ninety-nine singers had made it to this next level. Only sixty would survive the group round, and only forty-four would survive round three.

I tried not to think about the odds as I talked to others about joining into groups. I was thrilled when my miracle girl, Lauren, approached me immediately. Veronica, the girl who had wondered how I sounded, said she wanted to work with us. By the time another Chicago contestant, Elease, joined us, we had formed "Reziliance"—so named because no matter what they threw at us, we kept bouncing back! We chose "Band of Gold" as our song, and we worked on dance moves and harmony parts until nearly three in the morning.

When we arrived back at the hotel, I was annoyed to discover that my room key didn't work. I went down to the lobby to get a new key, but the man at the desk told me they were consolidating hotel rooms. Since my roommate had been eliminated, I'd have to move into another vacant spot . . . immediately! I had to pack all my stuff and move into another room, but when I got there, my new roommate, Tameka, was still practicing with another girl. She'd also left the Do Not Disturb sign on the door all day, so the room hadn't been cleaned.

Too exhausted to interrupt their rehearsal and not eager to sleep in a dirty bed, I went back to my old room and fell asleep at three-thirty. I set my alarm for five but received an unexpected wake-up call a half hour before the alarm went off. I rolled over and groaned, realizing that *American Idol* is a lot like boot camp . . . they really wanted to push us to our limits.

I wanted to snuggle my head into the pillow and go back to sleep, but I had work to do. My group had to rehearse. More exhausting than the rehearsal, though, was the knowledge that at any minute you could walk around a corner and find a television camera pointed in your direction. It's almost like knowing that "Big Brother" is watching—except he's not only watching, he might soon be *broadcasting* anything you say to a national audience.

From the time I made it downstairs to the moment Reziliance set foot on the stage, we rehearsed. Because I had watched the televised group round every season, I knew the judges would show no mercy to anyone who forgot the lyrics—

and we had chosen the "wordiest" song of the bunch! Debra Byrd, the vocal coach, informed us that each of us would sing both verses as a solo while the others sang "oohs" and "aahs" in the background. After going over our routine at least a hundred times, we finally felt ready.

Each group drew numbers to ascertain their performance order. Out of the thirty slots, we chose lucky number thirteen, then sat back to watch the first twelve ensembles.

Uh-oh. After watching the judges react to the groups that went ahead of us, we decided they were not in a good mood. Despite our misgivings, we strolled onto the stage. After a brief introduction by Elease, we began to sing.

Elease, soloing first, got flustered and forgot her words in the middle of the first verse. She eventually picked up the lyrics, but the damage had been done.

My heart contracted in sympathy when Elease twirled to her background position and Veronica took center stage. Sure enough, during the second verse, she forgot her words too. When she turned to look at us for help, I sang the lyrics to help her get back on track. She finished up with a bang, but the judges had seen her slip.

Next up was Lauren. She knew this song better than anyone, and her performance was flawless. Every word, every note, every dance move was perfect.

I knew I had a lot to measure up to as I pranced to center stage. I soared into the first verse and improvised on the melody to distinguish my performance from the others. So far, so good, and I was feeling confident.

Until the second verse. Wise old Solomon knew what he was talking about when he said pride goes before destruction and haughtiness before a fall. I fumbled my words, but I managed to cover my mistake by what I like to refer to as the "Mandisa remix." No one but folks who knew the song would have realized that I made up new lyrics, but the judges probably knew the song.

Knowing I couldn't go back and fix anything, I decided to leave the judges on a high note, so I did. As I circled around to join my three counterparts, I saw Simon hold up his hand, indicating that he'd seen enough. We ignored him because we had worked really hard on our big finish and we were determined to let the judges see it. As we shimmied our way to our positions, we ended our mediocre performance with a resounding *boom kack* and held our final pose.

At least we ended well.

When we finally broke our pose, I felt certain Lauren would be the only one from our group to advance. Elease, Veronica, and I had all flubbed the words, a nearly unpardonable sin in this round.

The judges immediately voiced their opinions. Randy began by saying that our group was split right down the middle. He said Elease and Veronica had really messed up and he suspected that Lauren and I had sung "Band of Gold" before. I sighed in relief, because he must not have noticed how I messed with the lyrics.

Paula said I was great and Lauren was fantastic. In her usual encouraging way, she commended the other two for how beautiful they looked, but agreed that they had dropped the ball. With positive comments from both Randy and Paula, I was beginning to feel confident that Lauren and I would advance to the next round.

Until we heard from Simon. He began by saying that I was the best of the four but that wasn't saying much. "Mandisa—"

he looked me in the eye—"if you had performed like that yesterday, I'm not sure you would be here now."

I blinked, stunned by the way he had stomped on my rising hope. He said something about Lauren doing well technically but missing something he called "the X factor." After he berated Elease and Veronica for forgetting the lyrics, he bent toward Paula and Randy. The three of them deliberated in whispers for a few minutes while the four of us stood like convicted murderers dreading a potential death penalty. I'm convinced that Randy, Paula, and Simon were not really saying much to each other. I think they just wanted to torture us a while.

After what seemed like an eternity, the judges looked up at Elease. Randy sighed. "I'm sorry. You're going home."

Next, Paula addressed Veronica. "I'm sorry, sweetheart. You will not be moving on."

I was surprised by the order, but Randy spoke to me next. "You're moving on to the next round."

The crowd behind the judges cheered, and I nearly melted in relief. I was convinced Lauren would also be moving on, but to my dismay, Simon announced that she would be going home.

My jaw dropped as Lauren gracefully composed herself and walked off the stage with the rest of us. We entered the theater lobby where the cameras waited to capture our reactions. Again, it was hard for me to celebrate when my friends had just been sent home. I knew I wasn't giving the producers "good TV," but at that moment I didn't care about the show's entertainment value.

My Reziliance counterparts had to face the disappointment of rejection, and I had to face the less painful but still awkward realization that I'd been advanced.

As I mentally rehearsed what had happened, I overheard one contestant and her mom talking about how the producers were advancing "pretty people who can't even sing." They weren't referring to me—they were talking about what they called the "tall, white, blonde" girls who had also forgotten their words.

I tried not to get involved in that discussion, but I couldn't help but wonder why Lauren had been sent home when she did a better job than I did. In the end I realized that music—most art, in fact—has a subjective element. Two singers, two painters, two writers can all follow the rules and produce sound, good work; but one song, one painting, one book pleases a judge while its competitor does not.

Since there was no possible way to predict how any judge would react on any given day, more than ever I realized that while I still needed to do my best, ultimately God was in control of my situation.

Out of the Fishbowl, into the Sea

As the pool of contestants grew smaller, the sense of competition grew keener. I wasn't comfortable with the vibe, and I didn't want to compete with the people who were becoming my friends; yet I knew that *American Idol* was a lot like *Survivor*—the game required a certain amount of strategy.

For the most part my fellow contestants smiled and acted friendly, but it wasn't unusual to hear gossip and backbiting. I was accustomed to support and loving acceptance from fellow musicians, so again I felt like a fish out of water.

But the Lord had brought me to that place, so I determined that while I would do what I could to be a worthy contestant, I would not resort to gossip or playing head games in an attempt to intimidate others. I'd simply press on and try to glorify Christ.

After the group competition we entered round three, an a cappella performance. From a list of songs, I chose Bonnie Raitt's "Something to Talk About." After letting us practice a while, the *Idol* staffers sent us back to the hotel, where I learned that my latest roommate, Tameka, had been eliminated.

I was beginning to feel like Typhoid Mary, infecting everyone in my vicinity—everyone I came close to seemed to get cut. Before she left, Tameka and I talked about the purposes and plans of the Lord. She was a mature believer, so she handled her disappointment really well. Impressed with her maturity, I said goodnight and drifted off to sleep with the weight of the next day's events looming over me.

After breakfast the next morning, we headed to the theater for our final Hollywood audition. I pulled number twenty-three out of sixty and was grateful I'd be getting my performance out of the way in the first half of the day. This round would be particularly tense because for the first time we wouldn't receive any comments from the judges. We would simply sing our song and walk off the stage. It would be hours before we'd learn whether or not we had advanced to the top forty-four.

Simon began by telling us that our slates had been wiped clean and we would be judged only on this final audition. The judges would not take our previous performances into consideration.

I wasn't sure how I felt about his statement. I'd turned in two fairly strong performances, but I was also feeling confident about my rendition of "Something to Talk About." I had given it some soul and arranged the melody to highlight the best parts of my voice.

When my turn came, I sauntered onto the stage and subtly graced into "People are talkin', talkin' 'bout people . . . "

Then my mind went as blank as paper. I don't know what was going on in my brain, but the lyrics that should have been on the tip of my tongue had been moved to deep storage. I tried to improvise with familiar snatches of phrases and ended up confusing the verses and completely losing my place. I thought I did a decent job of fudging the words, but I knew my cover was blown when Randy looked up from his paper with his eyes about to pop out of his head.

I'd planned to showcase my range on the chorus, but Simon lifted his hand before I got that far. I clamped my mouth shut and stared at him, unable to believe what had happened. Was that it? Was I finished?

I slumped off the stage, knowing I'd turned in my worst performance yet. I walked into the lobby and told the guys filming post-audition interviews that if Simon had been honest about judging us on this performance only, I was headed home.

By the time I finished my interview, the contestants, staff, and crew took a lunch break. Too discouraged to eat, I retreated to the holding room to sulk.

As I sat there by myself, I struggled to shake off the feeling of dread that felt like a weight on my shoulders. I had done so well all week, and now everything was coming to an end. How *could* I have forgotten those words?

When my stomach began to complain of hunger, I headed downstairs to the catering room, grabbed a sandwich, and gulped it down. I ate alone, and as I ate, I could feel sharp stares pricking my spine. Had everyone seen the mess I'd made? The words of my song came back to haunt me—were they all talking about me?

Ashamed and embarrassed, I headed back up to the holding room, then sat alone and listened to my iPod. While the final thirty contestants auditioned, I dozed fitfully on a bench, waking only when someone shook me and said they were moving us to the hotel to await the judges' final decision.

Even though I was sure what my fate would be, I was committed to staying for every meeting. Otherwise I'd have been in a cab and on my way to LAX for the first available flight back to Nashville.

But I was stuck for the duration.

Reservation for One at the Party of Praise

On the bus ride to the hotel, I slipped my iPod's earbuds into my ears and listened as Yolanda Adams began to serenade me with the words from "Open My Heart": *Alone in a room, it's just me and you.*

Reminded of my spiritual reality, I began to worship the Lord on the bus, and I continued to pray as we entered the hotel holding room. I sat in a quiet corner as we waited for the judges to arrive and deliver their verdict.

I wanted to sit alone and focus on worshipping God, but producers and cameramen roamed the room, trying to capture the intensity of these tense moments. We were told to sit quietly and think about what might happen next, and the cameras caught every emotion that ran across our faces: worry, fear, anxiety—all of it.

They didn't have to direct me; I was way ahead of them. In fact, I didn't pay them much attention, because the Lord and I were having a serious discussion of our own. With the help of

Michael W. Smith's recording of "Draw Me Close," I continued to pour out my heart to Jesus, inwardly singing,

> *You're all I want.*
> *You're all I've ever needed.*
> *You're all I want.*
> *Help me know you are near.*

I told God that no matter what happened, I would trust Him. He *was* all I needed. As I considered God's faithfulness through the years, I began to tear up . . . and before long a smile spread over my face. Anyone watching me must have thought I was delirious.

In that quiet corner, the Lord lifted my anxious burden. Along with Travis Cottrell's worship team on the CD, I lifted my heart in song:

> *I'm trading my sorrows. I'm trading my shame.*
> *I'm laying them down for the joy of the Lord!*[1]

Like unblinking eyes the cameras around me searched for serious, intense, and worried expressions. They merely grazed over me, because in my little corner I was having a praise party. I was clapping my hands and singing full throttle in my heart, lifting my praises to the Lord.

God had freed me from the cares of the competition, and I felt peace about whatever the day's outcome might be. In that hour the Lord taught me how to worship Him in the midst of sorrow and fear, and I wanted to remember the lesson for the rest of my life.

My worship jubilee came to an end as someone announced the judges' arrival. Executive producer Ken Warwick entered the room and told us they would be dividing us into four separate groups. The first set of names he would read should go to room number 2.

He pulled out a sheet of paper and began reading from the top: "Mandisa Hundley. . . ." As I walked to the front of the room, I listened as he read the other names. All fourteen of those other contestants had done an exceptional job that week, so I began to feel confident about making it into the elite forty-four.

As the Lord would have it, my instinct was right. The fifteen of us sat in a private room as the judges came in to tell us that we represented one third of the chosen group. We celebrated with tears, hugs, and screams of joy. Later we gathered in a larger room with all the remaining contestants, grateful that the stressful week had finally come to an end. After a final day of interviews and photo shoots, we would disband and go home.

I found myself thinking of Nashville . . . and realizing that it felt like another world. Time had stopped since I'd left, and soon I'd have to go home and pick up where I'd left off.

How could anyone do that?

> I found myself thinking of Nashville . . . and realizing that it felt like another world. Time had stopped since I'd left, and soon I'd have to go home and pick up where I'd left off. How could anyone do that?

And Life Goes On

Once we got home, we would have to resume our normal lives as if nothing had changed. We'd have to sit around our Christmas dinner tables and smile at our families as if we weren't about to burst with news about everything that had happened in California.

The audition shows wouldn't begin to air until January, and we wouldn't know if we'd been chosen to be in the top twenty-four until even later. One of the producers explained that the judges would meet in January to whittle the group of forty-four down to twenty-four, twelve men and twelve women. Without any additional songs from us, they would review our performance tapes and consider audience reaction as well as our talent and skill. The top twenty-four names would be announced on February 15, and the semifinals would begin right after that announcement.

For self-employed people like me, the stop-and-start aspect of *American Idol* can be incredibly frustrating. Unlike many of the other contestants, I wasn't in school or relying on my parents for financial support. I was older, and I'd been supporting myself for several years. If I didn't work, I didn't eat, *and* I had student loans to pay and an apartment in Nashville to maintain. I had to find some kind of work so I could survive.

When I returned to Nashville, I tried to ease back into my old life. I took session jobs if they came up, but a lot of the income I'd been hoping for didn't—*couldn't*—come in because I had to shut my Web site down, and that prevented me from selling my CD. Without a Web site or the opportunity to release and sell my new CD, I knew my finances would soon be in sorry shape.

One night not long after returning home, I was lying in bed trying to sleep. My mind kept racing, and suddenly I realized I needed to look up my checking account balance. I called my bank's twenty-four-hour information line and listened in horror as the automated female voice politely told me my balance was *negative* two hundred dollars.

How in the world? What had I been buying? I realized I'd

fallen victim to the ease of using a debit card—swipe it and buy it—and I'd neglected to record every purchase. To save money, I'd been cutting corners in every way I knew, but no matter how you economize, the rent still comes due every month.

I didn't want to ask my parents for money—I suppose pride prevented me—but I didn't know what else I could do. I wasn't supposed to tell people about my status with *Idol,* so I couldn't explain that I was still in the competition and unable to work with any kind of regularity.

In the darkness of that night I crept to my computer and I typed out an e-mail. I have a small group of friends that I call intercessors because they frequently offer prayers, petitions, and entreaties to the Lord on my behalf. They're real prayer warriors, and they had a pretty good idea of what was happening in my life.

I believe in prayer because I have seen the results of effective prayer in my own life. The way I look at it, prayer is simply communicating with God. Whenever I speak to my best friend, Chandra, we talk about all kinds of things—what is happening in my life, her life, things we are worried about, things we are thankful for. We laugh about old memories, anticipate things to come, and make future plans.

Just as I communicate with Chandra, I communicate with God. Notice I said *communicate,* not just *speak to.* Communication goes two ways. I don't think Chandra and I would have a very pleasant relationship if I talked only about myself without giving her a chance to speak! The key to good communication is speaking *and* listening. Maybe God was trying to illustrate a point when he gave us *two* ears and only one mouth.

Through prayer, God invites us to play an active role in our faith walk. I believe He listens to our petitions and makes things happen as a result of our faith working through our prayers. The Bible tells us to pray for each other and promises that "the earnest prayer of a righteous person has great power and produces wonderful results" (James 5:16). Because of that promise, I know it's important to surround myself with people who I know will pray for me.

I sent my praying friends an e-mail and simply let them know I had an opportunity and a need. Most of those folks had told me to let them know if they could help in any way, so I swallowed my pride and asked for their support. Within a day or two, my intercessors, my parents, and other family members began to send financial gifts that more than satisfied my need.

I don't know what I'd have done without them. They not only prayed for me and loved me, but they were also willing to open their wallets as well as their hearts.

With my financial needs met and Hollywood week behind me, I began to feel more confident about my chances on *American Idol.* I didn't want to win—I honestly didn't see myself as American Idol material—but I began to believe that maybe God meant for me to make it into the top ten, maybe even the top three.

> I had no idea what Simon had said to the cameras after I had left the room . . . and what he'd soon tell the world.

After all, my fellow contestants had befriended me; the producers liked me; and Paula, Randy, and Simon loved me . . . or so I thought.

But I had no idea what Simon had said to the cameras after I had left the room . . . and what he'd soon tell the world.

5 Tender Mercies

January 17, 2006, marked the premier of the fifth season of *American Idol*. The debut episode would feature auditions from Chicago, my audition city. I knew I'd already been selected for the top forty-four but was excited because I'd finally be able to break my silence.

I didn't know if they'd air my audition, but I had a strong feeling they would because I had seen commercials featuring my triumphant exit from the audition room. My friends Chance and Jennifer Scoggins offered to host an *American Idol* premier party for me, and Jennifer had spread a marvelous feast on the table and lit candles throughout the house. Everyone was in a festive mood, especially me.

More than twenty of my closest friends gathered at the Scogginses' to watch the premier. Chance decided to record the show with his TiVo so we wouldn't have to sit through the commercials. So we waited a while and snacked on the delicious feast, laughing and talking about how we had all been anticipating this night. I've always said that I have to be the world's leading *American Idol* junkie, but Travis and Chance could definitely contend for the title. I knew how proud this night would make them.

I was jazzed because I remembered that first audition clearly, and I'll never forget how impressed the judges had been. Paula, Randy, and even Simon had been complimentary and appreciative . . . and I was eager to let the world eavesdrop on my experience.

When everyone had eaten, we settled in the family room to watch the show. People crowded onto the sofa and perched on the edges of chairs, craning their necks for a clear view of the television screen. Several folks stretched out on the floor, as comfortable as family.

I sat in a comfortable chair, feeling a little like show-business royalty because Chance had "crowned" me with a plastic tiara. Chance and Jennifer had also surprised me by printing almost a hundred brown T-shirts that said "Mandisa Is My American Idol—All Hail the Diva" beneath a shining star.

I had laughed when they answered the door wearing those shirts, but I couldn't deny that I'd been touched by their sweet faith in me.

My nerves tightened when the show began. My pulse quickened as the familiar logo flashed across the screen, and I almost pinched myself to make sure I wasn't dreaming. Even now I found it hard to believe that I'd been there; I had *talked* to Ryan Seacrest and laughed with Paula and Randy. I knew those people on the television screen, and wonder of wonders, they knew me.

The little girl had finally found the courage to stand up, leave the house, and take a risk. *Thank You, Lord!*

The show began, and we enjoyed watching the good and not-so-good performances. Several moments were so funny that we had to stop and rewind so we could enjoy them again.

Whenever possible I took a moment to share behind-the-scenes stories about certain contestants after their auditions were featured. Amazement lit the shining eyes that turned toward me—my friends were just as fascinated by this adventure as I was.

As the minutes ticked by, I kept glancing at the clock and wondering when they were going to show my audition. I barely noticed when the phone rang, but Chance pulled himself off the couch to answer it. A moment later I saw him signaling for my attention. I felt a fleeting second of irritation—whatever it was, couldn't it wait? Then I realized that Chance wouldn't interrupt me unless something really important had come up.

I excused myself and stood. "Should we stop the recording?" someone asked, but I shook my head. May as well let them keep watching.

Chance pulled me aside and drew a deep breath. "That was Kevin on the phone," he said. "They're watching the show in real time. You just sang."

I lifted a brow. "So?"

"So after you left the room, Simon said something rude about your weight."

I stood stock-still as despair sucked all the air out of the room. Tears stung my eyes, and a sob stuck in my throat. Chance's expression softened; he knew I was struggling to put on a brave face. My emotions had been at an unusually high pitch all day, so it didn't take much to send them plummeting in the opposite direction.

I glanced at the front door. What would people think if I walked out and didn't come back? I didn't want to have to deal with this, especially not in front of my friends, but I couldn't be rude to Chance and Jennifer.

I took a deep breath, thanked Chance for the warning, and went to join the others in the family room. I must have looked like a zombie, but they didn't notice. They were really into the show, because my face had finally filled the screen—they were airing some of my interview with Ryan.

I pressed my lips together and tried to keep my chin from quivering. That day had been so good; why had Simon gone and ruined it?

The camera shifted and showed me singing "Fallin'."

When I'd finished only a few lines of the song, the judges stopped me. The cameras showed Paula, Randy, and Simon saying nice things and counting down together as they sent me through to the Hollywood round. The camera zoomed in on my beaming face, then showed me leaving the room in a joyous conniption fit.

> Before a national television audience, Simon looked at Paula and asked, "Are we going to get a bigger stage this year?"

My friends erupted into cheers and applause. Few of them were watching the screen when the camera zoomed in on Simon again, but those who looked at my face quickly turned their attention back to the television.

Before a national television audience, Simon looked at Paula and asked, "Are we going to get a bigger stage this year?"

Paula slapped him playfully and said I reminded her of

Frenchie Davis, a former contestant. Simon grinned cheekily and said, "She's more like *France*."

I swallowed hard and tried to smile when the friends who'd heard these comments turned to look at me. "Oh, it's okay," I said, my voice wobbling. "I'm okay."

Those who'd been celebrating went dead silent as the others stared at me. I lowered my gaze, not knowing how to react. I'd gone from my life's highest moment to one of its lowest, and I'd had to do it under the watchful eyes of my closest friends.

But they were compassionate friends. "Simon's a jerk," someone said, and immediately others moved in to embrace me.

I accepted their words of sympathy, but I wanted to turn and run . . . or maybe hide in a closet until everyone had left. When I'm hurt, the introvert in me wants to retreat and lick my wounds, and this occasion was no exception. After so many good things, to be left with this bitter moment . . . it didn't seem fair.

We watched the rest of the show, but the gathering now felt more like a funeral wake than a party. Those "All Hail the Diva" T-shirts sprinkled throughout the room seemed to mock me.

When the closing credits rolled across the screen, my friends Fiona, Tammy, and Alicia pulled me away from the others to share a word of encouragement.

"What Simon did was horrible," Fiona said. "But just think of what could be going on right now in the heavenlies."

In a corner of the family room, all three of them held on to my hands and arms and prayed with me. Fiona prayed for my aching heart and asked the Lord to help me forgive Simon. She said this situation was about more than me, it was about Simon and how through my hurt maybe he could catch a glimpse of the Lord Jesus.

Sounded like a pretty tall order to me.

As I drove home from Chance's house, my feelings still raw and aching, I saw a flashing light in my rearview mirror. I turned into a gas station and groaned inwardly. *What next, Lord? Hasn't this night been bad enough?*

The policeman came to my window and told me one of my taillights was out—a traffic infraction. I sighed and said I was sorry but I didn't know. My car had been on its last legs for a long time. . . .

He nodded without smiling. "May I see your license and registration?"

I reached across the car and fumbled at the glove box for my registration, then pulled my license from my wallet. My emotions were still barely under control, but I pressed my lips together and tried to remain calm. I didn't want to start sobbing in front of a cop.

I gave him my papers, and he walked back to his car.

Great. I ran my hands over the steering wheel and wondered what else could go wrong in a single night. Maybe I'd have a flat tire a few miles down the road. Maybe my apartment had burned down while I was out. Maybe someone had stolen my ID and this cop was going to come back and tell me I was a wanted woman in fourteen states. . . .

I lifted my head as I heard footsteps approaching. The cop paused outside my window and returned my license and registration. "So—where are you coming from, a friend's house?"

I blinked in confusion, then nodded.

"Out celebrating your premier on *American Idol*?"

Amazed, I nodded again. "How did you—"

"I just came on duty," he explained. "And I saw you. You were good, and we were cheering for you." He touched his hand to his brow in a light salute. "Because you're a star, I'm going to let you go with a warning. You take care, and be sure to get that taillight fixed, okay?"

He walked away, and as I turned the key to urge my pitiful car back to life, I felt the peace of God wash over me in a warm and caressing tide. *I'm with you, I'm for you, and this process is going to be good. Wait and see.*

A Living Tapestry

Over the next few days, as I thought about my predicament and begged God for a forgiving spirit, I remembered a passage of Scripture that seemed especially apt in my situation:

> Though I am the least deserving of all God's people, he graciously gave me the privilege of telling the Gentiles about the endless treasures available to them in Christ. I was chosen to explain to everyone this mysterious plan that God, the Creator of all things, had kept secret from the beginning.
>
> God's purpose in all this was to use the church to display his wisdom in its rich variety to all the unseen rulers and authorities in the heavenly places. This was his eternal plan, which he carried out through Christ Jesus our Lord.
>
> Because of Christ and our faith in him, we can now come boldly and confidently into God's presence. So please don't lose heart because of my trials here. I am suffering for you, so you should feel honored. (Ephesians 3:8-13)

I began to realize that my trial with Simon—which paled in comparison to the trials Paul had endured—might have a higher purpose. I kept thinking of Joseph, the son of Jacob who was sold into slavery by ten of his brothers. At the end of his long trial, when he found himself face-to-face with brothers who didn't even recognize him, he said, "What you intended for evil, God intended for good."

I didn't think Simon was evil—thoughtless, maybe, and mean—but maybe God could find a way to bring real good out of comments that had brought me nothing but misery. I smiled as I considered the possibilities—what might happen if Simon became a radical believer in Jesus? The entertainment world could be turned upside down.

> I didn't think Simon was evil—thoughtless, maybe, and mean—but maybe God could find a way to bring good out of comments that had brought me nothing but misery.

I was even beginning to see how blessed I was to be among friends when Simon's comments aired. If I'd known what he was going to say, I would have stayed home and watched the show by myself. Then I would have sulked for days, if not weeks. Inevitably I would have driven through the Krispy Kreme drive-through and soothed my sorrows with a dozen hot glazed donuts. The next morning I would have awakened and felt horrible, awash with shame and guilt. After so many hours of feeling terrible, I would have indulged in a medium Papa John's pizza and a gallon of Purity's Caramel Pie ice cream. I would have cried myself to sleep that night and begun the vicious cycle again in the morning. . . .

I would be a little girl again, secure on my couch and surrounded by my comfort foods, afraid to risk hurt and ridicule.

But God knew what I needed. Because I was with Christian friends the night of the premier, my pain was eased almost immediately. Fiona, Tammy, and Alicia surrounded me in prayer and reminded me of what was important. My hurt feelings weren't that big a deal—lots of people get their feelings hurt every day, and they survive.

The important thing, the crucial difference, was that I'd been mocked and insulted on national television. I would never have chosen to have my audition end that way, but my sovereign Lord allowed Simon to say what he did. Jesus knew the cameras were rolling . . . and He knew the world would be waiting and watching for my reaction.

> Jesus knew the cameras were rolling . . . and He knew the world would be waiting and watching for my reaction.

Through the next few days, the words of Psalm 37:23-24 came back to encourage me: "The LORD directs the steps of the godly. He delights in every detail of their lives. Though they stumble, they will never fall, for the LORD holds them by the hand." So did these words from Psalm 139:15: "You watched me as I was being formed in utter seclusion, as I was woven together in the dark of the womb."

The words *woven together* in Psalm 139 come from a Hebrew word that refers to a skillful embroiderer, someone who takes great pains with many colored threads to create something beautiful. That's what God does. He creates our bodies and grants us natural personalities while gifting us with unique tendencies and talents. In His infinite, sovereign wisdom, He created me with black skin, dark eyes, a pear-shaped body, a sweet tooth, and a musical voice. He gave me flaws as well as gifts, and I've learned to praise Him for everything He has given.

The psalmist used the metaphor of embroidery and weaving to describe God's work because life is a tapestry. In order to highlight the moments of gold and silver, you have to include dark threads for contrast. A patch of gold doesn't attract much attention on a field of white, but it glows like a beacon against a dark background.

After I'd had time to reflect on Simon's comments, I began to see the gold and silver threads in the darkness of my *American Idol* premier. I began to count them: First, Simon's comments might make people more sympathetic toward me as a contestant. Second, Simon had handed me a gift-wrapped opportunity to publicly demonstrate forgiveness and reflect the love of Christ. Third—and this was the hardest to recognize and accept—Simon's comments became the impetus I needed to kick-start my plan to live a more healthful lifestyle and get my eating under control.

> Simon's comments became the impetus I needed to kick-start my plan to live a more healthful lifestyle and get my eating under control.

Food, Glorious Food

Food has always been a problem for me. Over the years I've tried every diet you can name: Weight Watchers, Jenny Craig, NutriSystem, Atkins, Slim-Fast. I lost weight on each of those plans, but inevitably the weight came back because diets are temporary. Living thin requires a lifestyle change—a change I wasn't ready to make a permanent part of my life.

I know the best weight-reduction programs are those that take weight off slowly through a combination of good eating and exercise. The slower a person takes weight off, the more likely he or she is to keep it off, because the person is forming good nutritional habits. Anyone—including me—can starve for a couple of days to lose a couple of pounds, but unless we change our destructive patterns, we'll only regain the weight—and a couple of other pounds to keep it company.

I also know that dieting—or eating a restricted diet of less than twelve hundred calories a day—slows the body's metabolism so that it actually burns fewer calories per day, making it even *harder* to lose weight. Along with the minimum twelve hundred calories, a sedentary person also needs regular physical exercise to keep the body's engine revved up to performance speed.

See how well I know the lingo? I know the facts about metabolism and food. I also know that my food addiction is the outward manifestation of a deep inner issue. To beat this addiction, I'm going to have to discover and confront the reasons I turn to food for comfort.

Confronting the issue is easier said than done. Some issues are deep, and some are so covered over by time and indifference and pretense that they're painful to bring to the surface.

Facing the Pain of the Past

I don't think I've uncovered all my issues yet, but I know that one of the reasons I'm addicted to food stems from my family situation. Because my parents divorced when I was two, I've often struggled with feelings of rejection from my father. My head knows Dad loves me, and he says it every time we speak, but I can't forget how my childish heart kept wondering why he left me and Mom. I was too young to understand everything that can go wrong in an adult relationship, so like most kids of divorce, I thought I had something to do with their breakup. Somehow, in some way, I wasn't good enough, so that's why Dad left.

Those feelings of rejection didn't fade away after the divorce. Because Mom had to work throughout my childhood, I spent a lot of time alone, and food was always a good friend. Eating gave me something to do, brought me pleasure, and made me feel satisfied. Food became the substitute that—literally—filled the empty places within me.

The other day I looked through some old pictures from my childhood and realized that I didn't get heavy until I was about ten years old—not coincidentally, that was the time when my father's family moved east, ending my twice-a-month visits. Before that time I was an active kid—I used to be quite a runner. On weekends at my dad's house, I remember racing against kids from the neighborhood. I was so fast! My half brother, Bryan, would have me race his friends, who couldn't believe that a little girl could beat them.

After Dad and his family left the area, however, I began to really pack on the pounds. At first I ate to stuff my emotions, and after a while overeating became a habit. No matter what emotion I had to deal with, my immediate reaction was to turn to food.

One of my best friends from junior high school was Kim, a beautiful Asian girl with long brown hair and almond-shaped eyes. She had a great figure and knew how to show it off. She often wore tight jeans and a low-cut top (conveniently covered with a sweatshirt until after she left her house).

I liked Kim a lot, even though she was involved in some questionable activities. She cut school, smoked, drank, and went too far with boys that were too old for her. But I felt cool when I hung with Kim, and every kid at that age wants to feel accepted.

By that time I had gained quite a bit of weight, but I tried to keep up with Kim by wearing really cute skirts. Most girls wore leg warmers underneath (remember, it was the eighties!), but because I felt insecure about my thick legs, I wore stretch pants beneath my skirts. I looked a mess, but ignorance is bliss.

One day after school Kim and I stepped off the bus in our neighborhood. As we walked the short distance to our houses, Kim pulled out a cigarette and lit up. For the first time, she offered me a puff.

I crinkled up my nose and said, "No, thanks," but Kim insisted I try it.

"Why?" I asked. "Why do you smoke?"

"It relaxes me." She shrugged and tossed her dark hair. "It'd relax you, too."

Curious, I took the smoldering cigarette and asked her what to do. She gave me a brief lesson in how to smoke, and then I put the cigarette to my lips. I inhaled a quick breath through the tobacco and immediately felt a scorching sensation at the back of my throat. I bent over, coughing and hacking, while Kim laughed.

Once I reached the safety of my house, I let myself in and ran to the kitchen, where I poured a large glass of orange juice and gulped it down. It soothed my throat a little, but I could still feel the burning sensation. So I poured myself a bowl of Honeycomb cereal and splashed on the milk, convinced the milk would glaze the seared tissues at the back of my throat.

When the milk and cereal didn't help, I mixed up a batch of Aunt Jemima waffle mix and cooked enough waffles for a family, then proceeded to eat every one. I didn't feel guilty in the least—after all, I'd been traumatized by my cigarette experience, so I deserved to eat.

Looking back, I realize now that Kim's addiction of choice was nicotine. Mine was breakfast!

My overeating habits became only more deeply ingrained as the years passed. Whenever something didn't go my way—and it didn't have to be a major thing—I'd make myself feel better by indulging in the pleasure of food.

My food addiction really spiraled out of control in high school. I don't like to talk about this, but when I was fifteen, a friend's neighbor raped me. I liked this boy. I enjoyed kissing him, but I didn't want to have sex with him. Like so many girls, I got caught in a situation and didn't know how to say *no* or *stop*. He squeezed my chest really hard and I couldn't get away; in that moment I felt like I was helplessly frozen.

Now I wonder why I didn't scream . . . now I wonder why I didn't tell someone right after it happened. I do remember feeling ashamed and guilty. I blamed myself for the incident, and that blame only reinforced my feelings of unworthiness and insecurity.

Now I can see that the rape wasn't my fault, but as a naive teenager with no real dating experience, I didn't know that I could have—*should* have—resisted more forcefully.

(Years later I saw my rapist, but he didn't recognize me. A friend told me that the man had overdosed on some drug and experienced complete amnesia as a result. I've often wondered if that was part of God's judgment against this man for his crime against me.)

The rape and its resulting guilt only made my food problem worse. I began to eat as a form of self-protection—maybe, I reasoned, if I cushion myself behind a layer of fat, men will leave me alone.

Now I can see exactly what I was doing—by letting the excess pounds drive men (and other people) away, I didn't have to risk facing the possibility that *Mandisa* might drive people away. I could guard my real self, my true personality; I wouldn't have to reveal myself and be found inferior. If I maintained a wall of flesh, I wouldn't have to lower my walls of self-protection.

Being an introvert worked against me too. For someone who "recharges" in solitude, the temptation to remain aloof from family, friends, and society was almost impossible to resist.

Much easier, by far, to sit on the sofa with a bowl of ice cream and a bag of chips. Much easier to watch TV and dream of being a singer than to get up and take a few wavering steps toward those dreams.

Tough Love Is Tough to Take

Many of my issues, ironically, are due to family members who made comments about my weight. Maybe they thought they were practicing tough love, but those comments hurt the most because they came from the people who were closest to me. I would pretend not to care or even not to hear (which probably only made them repeat their comments more loudly), but I can remember every remark:

"Your butt looks like a shelf."

"You're as big as a house."

At least I knew my family members loved me. I didn't have that assurance from people outside my family, and I heard plenty of comments at school, on the street, and on the bus. No wonder my idea of a perfect night was sitting at home in front of the TV!

I remember being on the drill team in high school. Our uniform consisted of sleeveless tops and short skirts—the combination looked cute on the other girls but was definitely not what I'd have chosen to wear.

One day we performed our routine at a pep rally in the school gym. After doing this move where we jumped up and then fell on the ground, I heard a section of students laughing in the bleachers.

Later I learned the reason for their laughter—a smart-aleck kid had made a crack about the gym shaking when *I* fell. I ran to the bathroom crying because he'd said that . . . and others had laughed. He'd said it to make a joke at my expense, and I couldn't believe anyone could be so mean and childish in high school.

> Until you discover the root of the food issue and deal with it, the weight will keep coming back.

After drying my tears, I went home and ate almost an entire box of Cheerios. Not until that moment did I feel comforted.

With all that was going on in my head and heart, no wonder my attempts at dieting were unsuccessful. Until you discover the root of the food issue and deal with it, the weight will keep coming back.

A Taste of Daniel

In January 2002, I decided to lose weight by following "Daniel's Diet." A group of friends had heard about the diet from Travis Cottrell's wife, Angela. She had done it as a cleansing process but assured me that I'd lose weight by following it.

Angela equipped me with books to read, menu plans, a shopping list, and a vegetable juicer. The plan revolves around healthy eating. For twenty-one days, you eliminate white flour, sugar, salt, meat, and dairy. You drink a lot of freshly juiced vegetables, primarily carrot juice, and eat mostly raw vegetables.

The diet seemed impossible, but I thought I could endure almost anything for only twenty-one days. So I stocked my refrigerator with carrots, lettuce, tomatoes, cucumbers, spinach, soy cheese, and soy milk, then set out on this new adventure.

By day three I was ready to quit. My face broke out in pimples, and I had a raging and persistent headache. Angela assured me that my body was only detoxifying and that the misery would pass after the first week.

She was right. By day eight I had energy to spare and had never felt better. The headache went away, and so did the pimples.

By day twenty-two I had lost thirteen pounds. As a reward, I treated myself to a large tub of buttered popcorn and a jumbo-sized package of M&Ms at the movie theater.

I woke up the next morning feeling sluggish and gross, so I decided to take the Daniel's Diet program for another twenty-one-day test drive. This time was easier, and I lost another twelve pounds. My clothes were looser and people began to notice my shrinking hips.

I loved the positive attention I was getting, so I stuck to the twenty-one-day diet for over a year. Between my three-week diet cycles, I would often reward myself with sweet treats for a couple of days; then I'd start the program again.

By the beginning of 2003, I had lost sixty pounds and dropped eight sizes. I *loved* shopping for new clothes. Men began to whistle and make eyes at me when I went out in public. Every now and then, one would be bold enough to approach and ask me for a date, and I was almost always eager to accept.

I enjoyed my share of fancy dinners, walks in the park, and even pushing men away when they came on too strong. I was feeling good about myself. More important, for the first time in my life I felt I was honoring the Lord in the area of food.

What? Didn't you know that overeating is a sin? Yes, I know there are quite a few overweight preachers, but I don't know any preachers who claim to be perfect. Gluttony is a lack of self-control in the area of food, and it can be as dangerous as other things we do to harm our bodies.

Paul wrote about this in 1 Corinthians 6:19-20: "Don't you realize that your body is the temple of the Holy Spirit, who lives in you and was given to you by God? You do not belong to yourself, for God bought you with a high price. So you must honor God with your body."

Scripture warns against overeating. Paul cautioned the Philippians about people whose "god is their appetite" (Philippians 3:19), and Solomon proclaimed that a wise person shouldn't "carouse with drunkards or feast with gluttons, for they are on their way to poverty" (Proverbs 23:20-21).

After losing sixty pounds, I stood before thousands of women at a Living Proof Live event and talked about my struggle with food. I spoke with authority, proclaiming that God had set me free in that area. I was living proof that if He could do it for me, He could do it for anyone.

Several women came up after that event to tell me that I had inspired them to do something about their weight. They identified with what I'd said and had jotted down all the inspiring Scripture references I had mentioned.

I came away feeling that I had made a difference. Imagine—me, a role model.

I couldn't believe it myself.

Shortly after that event, God called me to leave the comfort of my secure job at LifeWay and trust Him to provide for me after the iWorship tour. Needless to say, it was difficult to maintain the Daniel Diet while on the road. I was faithful to exercise nearly every day, but not many restaurants or caterers offer juiced carrots and raw vegetables. I tried to be faithful to the plan, but the beef, chicken, and dessert selections called to me like beloved friends in fond memories.

For three weeks I managed to stick to fruits and vegetables, but then I got a voice mail telling me that my godmother, Aunt Eula, had finally lost her long battle with cancer.

I hadn't seen Aunt Eula in years, but a few months before the tour she had attended a Living Proof Live event with my mom. Aunt Eula had enjoyed the first night but had been too weak to attend the second day. Mom and I were able to go to her house after the event, though, and spend time with her.

Aunt Eula was a soft-spoken woman who didn't mince words, but I had always known that she prayed for me. She took her duty as my godmother seriously, and at the darkest times of my life, I've always known that she was lifting my name to the Lord in prayer.

As I listened to my mom's message about Aunt Eula's funeral arrangements, tears filled my eyes. I was grateful the Lord had given us that time to spend with her only a few months before, but I couldn't help but grieve her loss. I knew she was in a better place, but I wanted her on earth, with me. Selfish, I know, but still . . .

What can I say? I caved.

I sat in silence for a while, then walked to the tour bus that would soon be leaving for the arena. During lunch, I ate three rolls with my chicken. Then I had a piece of chocolate cake. And a brownie. I'll be honest, those desserts tasted *wonderful*.

I excused my overindulgence by telling myself that I deserved a treat every now and then. But "every now and then" turned into "after every meal" within days.

By the end of the iWorship tour, I had spun back into my cycle of self-indulgence. To compound my problems, after returning to Living Proof Live events, I discovered that I wasn't able to sing as well as I used to. High notes that used to come easily became a struggle to reach.

In April 2003, I was at the First Baptist Church in Houston with Beth Moore and the praise team. We were doing a live simulcast featuring Beth's study *Beloved Disciple.*

I sang fine during the sound check. I sounded full voice as I did my vocal warm-ups. But when I began to sing a lead part on the song "In the Sanctuary," I opened my mouth and nothing came out. By the end of the event, Travis and Tammy were covering my parts . . . because my voice had vanished.

As the event concluded, I sat behind the stage and wept. What was happening? Was God taking my voice away permanently? Why now? I had just quit my job to work full-time in music.

I wiped tears from my cheeks and looked into the darkness behind the stage curtains. Was God trying to show me that I'd been full of pride? Was I not trusting Him enough? Should I stop doing these events? I had so many questions, and I wasn't hearing any answers.

I felt as if God had set me up for failure. For the next two weeks I dulled my anger and disappointment with candy, cheesecake, ice cream, hamburgers, french fries, milk shakes, cookies, tacos, nachos—if it was bad for me, I ate it.

On the Victory Road

By the beginning of 2004 I had regained all of my lost weight and then some. The Daniel Diet was great for losing weight, but I realized that until I dealt with the issues that kept me returning to food for comfort, I would never be able to maintain a healthy lifestyle permanently.

Now, more than a year after my first *Idol* audition, I'm dealing with my childhood issues and my insecurity. I'm watching what I eat, and I'm being careful to avoid eating too much white flour, sugar, and processed foods. I'm not into total deprivation (deprive yourself for long, and you'll open the gates for an indulgent binge), but I am eating lots of protein and vegetables and striving for a healthy balance. I have an exercise room in my house and love watching Joyce Meyer's *Enjoying Everyday Life* or Beth Moore on Wednesday's episodes of *LIFE Today* as I strut my stuff on my elliptical trainer or treadmill. I've also contacted a Christian therapist to help me resolve the issues that lie in my past.

When I heard Beth Moore talk about the pit from which the Lord had freed her, her experiential wisdom astounded me. "When dealing with temptation," she always said, "God is not asking if you can resist a year from now. He wants to know if you can resist *today*."

> It took *years* to put my weight on. My journey to a healthy weight will require more than a commitment of a few weeks. It will require a commitment to a healthy lifestyle, achieved one day at a time.

I know it took *years* to put my weight on. My journey to a healthy weight will require more than a commitment of a few weeks. It will require a commitment to a healthy lifestyle, achieved one day at a time.

Jesus put it this way: "Don't worry about tomorrow, for tomorrow will bring its own worries. Today's trouble is enough for today" (Matthew 6:34).

If we are faithful one day at a time, soon those days will turn into a week. Weeks will fade into months, and months into years.

Eventually I will be able to look back and say that God began the process of my deliverance when He accepted my prayer of repentance and adopted me as His daughter. I can look toward the finish line, when I will stand before my Savior after a lifetime of journeying in faith. Claiming the victory of that day, I can say, *Now I am free!*

In the meantime I am learning lessons that will help me remain healthy for the rest of my life. I have learned that periods of binging are a vicious cycle for me. Something sparks the binge, and I eat. Then I feel guilty for sinning against the Lord with my gluttony and lack of self-control, so in my shame, I ignore Him. But by ignoring Him, I close myself off from the help that can bring victory, the help that comes only from Him. Then I feel lonely and wretched, so I eat more, which keeps the cycle going.

This cycle has happened to me so many times that it has become habitual. Paul may not have been a glutton, but I'm convinced he dealt with something in his sin nature, because he writes eloquently about this struggle in Romans 7:18-25:

> I know I am rotten through and through so far as my old sinful nature is concerned. No matter which way I turn, I can't make myself do right. I want to, but I can't. When I want to do good, I don't. And when I try not to do wrong, I do it anyway. But if I am doing what I don't want to do, I am not really the one doing it; the sin within me is doing it."

It seems to be a fact of life that when I want to do what is right, I inevitably do what is wrong. I love God's law with all my heart. But there is another law at work within me that is at war with my mind. This law wins the fight and makes me a slave to the sin that is still within me. Oh, what a miserable person I am! Who will free me from this life that is dominated by sin? Thank God! The answer is in Jesus Christ our Lord. So you see how it is: In my mind I really want to obey God's law, but because of my sinful nature I am a slave to sin.

Face it, all diets work. Anytime we restrict our eating over a period of time, we can lose weight. But until we understand *why* we overeat, nothing will yield permanent results.

If you're trying to lose a few pounds, I would warn you to avoid unregulated weight-loss drugs. As I was writing this book, the Federal Trade Commission announced that it was fining the makers of Xenadrine EFX, CortiSlim, TrimSpa, and even One-A-Day Weight Smart vitamins for false advertising claims. In other words—they don't work.

"Testimonials from individuals are not a substitute for science," FTC Chairman Deborah Majoras told the Associated Press. "And that's what Americans need to understand." Majoras went on to say that consumer endorsers—those people you see in before-and-after photos—lost weight by rigorous diet and exercise programs.[1]

> Face it, all diets work. Any time we restrict our eating over a period of time, we can lose weight. But until we understand *why* we overeat, nothing will yield permanent results.

I always find it amusing to read the fine print beneath those photos. It usually says "results not typical."

If you're searching for a weight-loss program, I'd urge you to consider something you can follow for the *rest of your life.* Find something that allows you to enjoy the "forbidden foods" you love *on occasion,* and try to find something you can follow even when traveling or when eating with friends. I'm not going to endorse any specific program because so many good choices exist. But I know this—pounds come back on more easily than they slip off, so you will need to change your eating habits for life.

There are days when the bed feels so good that I miss my morning workout. There are other days when a television commercial ignites a desire for something I should avoid and I surrender to temptation.

But though eating right and exercising are important, I am learning that I must carry my temptations and struggles to the Lord rather than turn to food.

Sometimes I feel such a strong temptation for a certain food that I find myself rummaging through my cupboards in search of something similar. I have learned not to keep those "danger foods" in my house. If I want it, I will have to take the time to get dressed, get into my car, and drive somewhere to get it.

But during that time, the Lord will often get my attention. During my determined drive to the nearest convenience store, I will often realize that I am actually standing at an important crossroad. Faced with this realization, I recite Scripture in a clear and confident voice so that both I and the tempter can hear.

I firmly believe there is power in the spoken word, and I believe that power is limitless when we are speaking the Word of God. I will often walk around my house proclaiming, "The

Spirit of God, who raised Jesus from the dead, lives in you. And just as God raised Christ Jesus from the dead, he will give life to your mortal bodies by this same Spirit living within you" (Romans 8:11); or "You say, 'I am allowed to do anything'—but not everything is good for you. And even though 'I am allowed to do anything,' I must not become a slave to anything" (1 Corinthians 6:12).

I have been driving down the street when my senses were suddenly slammed by the image of the newest hamburger pictured in a fast-food restaurant window. (Those pictures can be downright pornographic, can't they? They are designed to arouse lust—a lust for food.)

My mind rationalizes, *I have been so good lately. I should reward myself by pulling into that drive-through.*

As I slant my car toward the turning lane, I continue in the same vein: *A hamburger is not complete without a large order of french fries and a milk shake. This one meal won't hurt. I'll begin my healthy eating plan tomorrow.*

Inevitably, unless "tomorrow" happens to be Monday, I will further stall my healthy eating plan because I'm sure it's written somewhere that all diets *have* to begin either on a Monday or on New Year's Day! (I have indulged in more "last suppers" on Sunday nights. . . .)

I will continue in this defeatist mode unless I change gears. Instead of surrendering to temptation, I can *choose to proclaim the living Word of God:* "The temptations that come into my life are no different from what others experience. And God is faithful. He will keep the temptation from becoming so strong that I can't stand up against it. When I am tempted, He will show me a way out so that I will not give in to it!" (1 Corinthians 10:13, paraphrased).

God's Word has gotten me out of several jams. Anytime I run across a Scripture verse that will help me in the fight, I jot it down on an index card and work on memorizing it. I am a living witness that God's Word *is* alive and powerful: "The word of God is alive and powerful. It is sharper than the sharpest two-edged sword, cutting between soul and spirit, between joint and marrow. It exposes our innermost thoughts and desires" (Hebrews 4:12).

I can't promise that if I were offered a magical pill to melt the weight off, I wouldn't take it. God can and does work through medicine to bring healing to His people. But until a genie floats out of the proverbial lamp, I will revel in the process, because I know victory does not lie just beyond the finish line—victory lies in the journey and in the lessons learned on the way.

> Do I want to look good, too? Sure, what woman doesn't? But my primary reasons for wanting to lose weight are not cosmetic; they're spiritual and health related.

Even though my weight problems have been dark threads in the tapestry of my life, I can see how God used them to bring me closer to Him. I was so hungry for love that when I heard about Jesus, I didn't hesitate to embrace Him as my Savior. And now, because I am hungry again—starving, really—for His approval, I want to embrace a healthy lifestyle so I can be a good steward of the life He's given me. I want my body to be a fit temple to be used in His service. I want to obey the verse that says, "Whether you eat or drink, or whatever you do, do it all for the glory of God" (1 Corinthians 10:31).

Do I want to look good, too? Sure, what woman doesn't? But my primary reasons for wanting to lose weight are not cosmetic; they're spiritual and health-related.

We Are Weight-Obsessed

Throughout my *Idol* experience I realized that weight has become a prevalent problem in America. Nearly everyone has problems with it, and few people will admit what a problem it is. I am always amazed when skinny women come up to me and tell me they struggle with food too. But I have learned that inner struggles are often disguised by outward appearances.

I remember one young friend of mine—she's a size zero—saying that she felt fat and needed to go on a diet. I couldn't believe what I was hearing. So many people today, especially young girls, are bombarded with unhealthy and unrealistic images that are routinely presented as a standard for beauty.

Did you know that as recently as the 1930s, some women swallowed pills containing tapeworms in order to stay slim? That may sound repulsive to you, but it's no more extreme than those who simply stop eating or resort to forced vomiting in order to prevent calories from being digested.

Women, we have to wake up and realize that the so-called standard we see in magazines is not real! Most models' photos are airbrushed to perfection. And have you ever considered why it's so difficult to become a fashion model? It's because models are *genetically unusual.* Most professional models are over 5 feet, 9 inches tall; have very small bones; and weigh about 123 pounds.[2] Those figures are anything but average.

According to the U.S. Department of Health and Human Services, the average U.S. woman is just under five feet, four inches tall and weighs 152 pounds.[3] The average adult American woman wears a size 14.[4]

The *Wall Street Journal* recently reported that Americans have bought into the myth that beauty is "natural" and some people achieve it without effort.

Excuse me while I snort in derision.

The truth is that few people are born with what we'd consider "natural" beauty—the rest of us have to work hard if we want to conform to society's standard.

The trick of being content and happy lies in learning how to live in a healthy body . . . and not in aspiring to look like some photographically altered woman in a magazine.

> The trick of being content and happy lies in learning how to live in a healthy body . . . and not aspiring to look like some photographically altered woman in a magazine.

The *Wall Street Journal* article reported that one popular magazine recently estimated that every year Jennifer Aniston spends "close to the average woman's annual salary" on trainers and other items related to keeping fit. Britney Spears told Oprah that she used to do between five hundred and one thousand crunches per day to keep her abs flat. And after having her baby, Kate Hudson worked out three hours a day to lose seventy pounds. The effort was so difficult that she used to sit on her exercise bike and cry.

"Entertainment figures and models," says the *Wall Street Journal,* "are like athletes; it takes a lot of discipline and social support to look like them. Money helps, too."[5]

Let's be honest: Would you rather spend three hours a day riding an exercise bike or taking a class learning to cook or laughing with your friends and family?

Not long ago I watched an episode of *Oprah* and saw a woman from another country talking about weight. She said—and I'm paraphrasing—that yes, people in America were heavier than in the country where she was from, but she couldn't help noticing that Americans were *obsessed* with weight. She said she was surprised to see so much emphasis on food in our media—a constant stream of ads for weight-loss programs, diet pills, the latest fad diet book, all juxtaposed against flashy fast-food commercials extolling the virtues of bigger and better burgers.

And that's another reason diets don't work permanently—they force you to think about food all day—what you *can* eat, what you *can't* eat, and *when* you can eat what you can.

I've been asked if I'd ever consider gastric bypass surgery, and recently I was tempted to do just that. After all, many people have lost weight after having this surgery, but I don't want to do it for a couple of reasons. First, while I believe such surgeries are tools you can use in your journey to fitness, I strongly believe that food is not the root problem. You will still have to deal with the issues compelling you to overeat. I've seen people lose weight with gastric bypass and substitute a new addiction for the old. Now that they can't overeat, they reach for alcohol; instead of food, they crave cigarettes.

Such substitutions are not healthy. You have to deal with issues at the root of your problem.

On *Idol*, I told the world I was "representin' for the big girls." I've never wanted to put my life on hold because I am not the size some record companies might want me to be. I know God made me beautiful, and I know He has given me a gift. As I travel down the path to better health, I am determined to live my life the best way I know how.

I want to spread a message of health, not vanity. Instead

of trying to measure up to a cosmetic standard, it's far more crucial for people to consider their health, their hearts, and whether they can walk up a flight of stairs without becoming winded. I also want people to know their worth is not dependent on their outward appearance. My value is not determined by my size, because beauty comes in *many* shapes and sizes.

No matter what your size, you can enjoy the beauty of confidence and inner peace. That sort of beauty is what I hope God and others see in me. It's what I wanted to display when I returned to *American Idol*.

> I want to spread a message of health, not vanity. I also want people to know their worth is not dependent upon their outward appearance. My value is not determined by my size because beauty comes in *many* shapes and sizes.

6 Troubles Surround Me

Seven days after Simon's comments about my weight aired, I had an opportunity to confront him face-to-face. Thirty million people had either seen him make those nasty comments or had heard about them, and everyone expected me to react. So I knew I'd have to.

On the twentieth of January, as I was having my daily devotional time in my Nashville apartment, the Lord spoke to me. It wasn't an audible voice, but the Holy Spirit guided me through the Word and revealed a verse that I recognized as a message meant for me.

I had been working through a First Place Bible study called *Seeking God's Best*, and the lesson for that day focused on consecration. I read Joshua 3:5: "Joshua told the people, 'Purify yourselves, for tomorrow the LORD will do great wonders among you.'"

In this age of hand sanitizers and *E. coli* bacteria, I'm sure I don't need to tell you what *purify* means. But the Hebrew word means more than "to sterilize"; it implies that the thing being purified should be ordained for holy use and handled with caution so it will remain free from defilement.

> Thirty million people had either seen him make those nasty comments or had heard about them, and everyone expected me to react.

After reading that verse, I felt the Lord calling me to consecrate myself by fasting and praying throughout the three days leading up to the moment I would face Simon and the rest of the judges. What I would say to Simon—my reaction to his insult—suddenly seemed ten times more important than knowing whether or not I had made it into *American Idol*'s top twenty-four.

I felt the weight of responsibility settle onto my shoulders. More than anything, I wanted to be a willing, purified vessel the Lord could use.

By January 23, when I flew back to Hollywood for the semifinals, I felt like a warrior approaching the battlefield. My friends back home were praying for me regularly. They were also praying *specifically:* They were asking the Lord to have mercy on Simon, to give me the grace to be able to forgive, and to grant me the wisdom to share that news with him.

Staffers herded the forty-four remaining contestants into a room and strategically seated us in rows. Ken and Nigel came out to prep us and said they wanted *lots* of reaction to what we'd seen when we watched our national premiers back home.

Then Nigel looked directly at me. "If Simon was a jerk, tell him off! We want a reaction."

I lifted a brow and assured him he would get one.

With the producers egging us on, we knew this was the beginning of a very long day. There would be no singing that day, just the walk we laughingly called "the green mile"—the long journey from the elevator to the small stool that waited before the judges' table.

What I would say to Simon—my reaction to his insult—suddenly seemed ten times more important than knowing whether or not I had made it into *American Idol*'s top twenty-four.

The procedure was simple: One person would go upstairs to meet the judges and hear whether or not he or she had made it into the top twenty-four, while someone else waited "on deck." Seven people went before me, and seven people came downstairs with sullen faces because they'd been cut. I was shocked when some of the strongest singers didn't make it through.

With each negative verdict, gasps echoed in the room, followed by hugs and teary farewells. Ambivalent feelings swirled in the atmosphere—we felt genuinely sorry for those who'd been cut, but each cut increased the odds that we remaining contestants would make it through.

Ryan Seacrest announced the next to walk the green mile: Katharine McPhee. Kat had caught my attention during the first round in Hollywood—I'm pretty sure my jaw dropped when I first heard the controlled, soulful voice that rolled out of her mouth. I expected the owner of such a voice to look like Beyoncé, Alicia Keys, or Mary J. Blige, but when I saw the stunning Caucasian beauty strut her stuff, I knew she was someone to watch. If *she* didn't make it through, I would be flabbergasted.

Ryan checked his list and continued: "On deck ... Mandisa."

Ouch—that worried me. So far they hadn't let anyone through, and I was certain Kat was a shoo-in. If they were being stingy with their approval, they probably wouldn't advance two people in a row.

Kat and I went into the room next to the elevator to prepare for the judges and get miked up.

Despite my noble intentions to take a stand for Christ before Simon, I was beginning to be distracted by the possibility I'd be cut before making the top twenty-four. As I waited for a sound technician to attach my microphone, Nigel came over to me.

"You know," he said, a sly smile curving his mouth, "you saw what Simon said about you."

I snorted softly. Who hadn't seen?

"We want you to say whatever you want to say to him," Nigel went on. "Don't even wait. As soon as you sit down, you just start talking and don't hold anything back."

"Don't worry," I said. "I've got some choice words for Simon."

I was pretty sure I knew what Nigel wanted me to say. Everyone in the room must have figured they knew what I wanted to tell the man who'd cut me so deeply. But I'd been praying about what to say for weeks. Nigel's not-so-subtle nudge reminded me of my most important mission.

I stepped onto the elevator and rose to the second floor. The camera on the elevator captured my brief prayer, then the sliding doors parted.

The Lord Will Do Great Wonders

I was feeling dry-mouthed as I walked the green mile, but I've never felt more determined. I moved into a large room that at first glance looked to be empty. No one spoke, so the only sound was the *thunk* of my boots on the hardwood floors. The sound made me feel heavy—and reminded me of Simon's comment—so I minced my way for a few steps, then gave it up.

I was a big girl, so I might as well walk like a big girl with style.

Halfway there . . .

In the distance to my right I saw Nigel, Ken, and a few other vaguely familiar faces. Some men were armed with cameras; others held long boom microphones to pick up every sound. Down front, bright lights burned behind thin scrims, illuminating what I'd already begun to think of as the hot seat.

I ran my hands over my shirt and slacks, checking to be sure I was fastened in all the proper places. I had chosen to wear a purple blouse with jewels on the front, hoping the stage lights would reflect the "bling" and lend an impression of sparkle and shine. If I was going home soon, I wanted to look good in my last appearance.

Almost made it. . . .

At the end of the green mile stood a large wooden table accented by three red Coca-Cola cups. Behind the table sat the three judges, all smiling. Behind the judges I could see large pictures of Kelly Clarkson, Fantasia Barrino, Carrie Underwood, and Ruben Studdard, previous *Idol* winners.

The last thing I saw was an itty-bitty chair beneath the lights. The hot seat was unbelievably *small.*

"Well, Simon," I called, continuing to stroll forward, "you didn't need a bigger stage, but you could have gotten me a bigger chair."

When Randy laughed and Paula smiled, I knew my comment had broken the ice, so I sat down and looked Simon square in the eye. "Simon, a lot of people want me to say a lot of things to you right now. But this is what I want to say—I want you to know that you hurt me. I cried, and it was very emotional for me. But the good thing about forgiveness is that you don't need someone to apologize in order to forgive them. So Simon, I want you to know I have forgiven you because if Jesus could forgive me for all the things I've done wrong, I can certainly extend that same grace to you."

When I began to speak, Simon looked over at Nigel with a *what's going on?* expression on his face. No one expected me to *forgive* Simon—they were expecting me to curse and scream at him like so many others had.

But as I delivered my message, Simon's smug grin disappeared. By the time I'd finished, he wore a look of shock and awe.

Behind me, so many people gasped that I felt air being sucked out of the room.

From the corner of my eye I saw Randy perk up and raise his brows. *"Wow,"* he whispered.

Paula's smile shone as bright as the lights overhead. I smiled, too, because I knew Jesus had breathed life into me and given me the courage to speak.

"Simon, a lot of people want me to say a lot of things to you right now. But this is what I want to say—I want you to know that you hurt me. I cried, and it was very emotional for me. But the good thing about forgiveness is that you don't need someone to apologize in order to forgive them. So Simon, I want you to know I have forgiven you because, if Jesus could forgive me for all the things I've done wrong, I can certainly extend that same grace to you."

In the silence that followed, Simon uncrossed his arms and hung his head. "Well, I feel about this big," he said, holding two fingers about an inch apart. "Mandisa, I'm humbled. Come here and give me a kiss."

Relieved, I stood to give him a hug, and he continued saying something about me catching him off guard. I knew it wasn't me who caught him by surprise but Jesus. He hadn't expected to encounter a Jesus example on the hot seat.

The remaining minutes of that interview are somewhat of a blur in my memory. Simon did all of the talking and tried to continue with the speech he'd planned before I interrupted. He was saying something about my being a session singer and did I have what it took to leave the background and move into the spotlight?

I barely heard him. My soul was singing, so I only half listened. I kept nodding, but my thoughts were far away, centered on a moment in Old Testament history. At a place called Ebenezer, the Philistines defeated the Israelites and captured the holy Ark of the Covenant (see 1 Samuel 4). Twenty years later, under Samuel's spiritual leadership, the Israelites defeated the Philistines at the same location:

> Just as Samuel was sacrificing the burnt offering, the Philistines arrived to attack Israel. But the LORD spoke with a mighty voice of thunder from heaven that day, and the Philistines were thrown into such confusion that the Israelites defeated them. . . . Samuel then took a large stone and placed it between the towns of Mizpah and Jeshanah. He named it Ebenezer (which means "the stone of help"), for he said, "Up to this point the LORD has helped us!"

> So the Philistines were subdued and didn't invade Israel again for some time. And throughout Samuel's lifetime, the LORD's powerful hand was raised against the Philistines. (1 Samuel 7:10-13)

Simon had landed a blow that wounded me deeply, and I had allowed myself to be vulnerable to his attack. But the Lord had given me courage, and through a simple message, He had thrown Simon into confusion.

As Simon talked, I was mentally stacking stones to build an altar of praise to the Lord.

I came back to reality when Simon gave me a sarcastic smile. "I'm afraid I *do* have bad news—you are going to have to put up with me for several more weeks because you are in the top twenty-four."

I screamed and slumped down in that little chair. All three of the judges stood, and I went down the line hugging Paula and Randy. When I saw Simon standing, I laughed and moved to embrace him. "Simon, you want *another* hug?"

"Why not?" he said, grinning. "We're practically dating now."

"You're not my type!"

As I walked out of the room, I was struck by an inexplicable wave of insecurity. I turned and glanced over my shoulder. "You guys aren't looking at my butt, are you?"

They weren't—at least, I hope they weren't.

In the elevator, I screamed, "Thank You, Jesus!"

The holding room was still buzzing from Kat's triumphant entrance, and I added to the excitement as I danced through the doorway and shouted out my happy news. I was embraced by a flurry of people, including my mom, who kept whispering, "Thank You, Jesus."

As I did an on-camera interview with Ryan Seacrest, I spotted Nigel as he came into the room. He walked toward me with a devilish grin on his face, then leaned over and whispered—in decidedly colorful language—that I was a superstar.

My Pain Redeemed

Now when I recall that episode, I think it epitomizes redemption. What the enemy meant for evil—to discourage me and destroy my hope—God meant for good. God brought something beautiful out of an ugly situation, and He continued to redeem it in the following weeks.

I don't believe I would have made it as far as I did in the *Idol* competition if Simon hadn't made those comments. His criticism endeared me to a lot of people, and people tend to vote for contestants with whom they can identify. Who hasn't been the victim of a rude or thoughtless comment at one time or another?

> Nigel walked toward me with a devilish grin on his face, then leaned over and whispered that I was a superstar . . . in decidedly colorful language.

The Lord graciously gave me the strength to say what I did to Simon, but you know the best part about that day? The producers filmed *and aired* every word of my comments.

As a huge fan of reality shows, I've noticed that Christians rarely come off looking good on network television. I remember watching the family edition of *The Amazing Race.* One contestant group professed to be Christians, but they spent a lot of time sniping at the others. On *America's Next Top Model,* the producers showed a self-proclaimed Christian contestant cursing at another girl. I know the film editors look for opportunities to exploit contestants' weaknesses, so during my *Idol* experience, I felt I needed to be extra careful lest anything I do be a bad reflection on the Lord.

That's a shame, because it's not the Lord who behaves badly in those high-stress situations, it's the people who claim His name. We are only human, but those who don't follow Christ are likely to look at those examples and assume that all Christians talk the talk without walking the walk. Or they think Christianity is centered on judgment, fire, and brimstone, and that's not an accurate picture either. If someone doesn't actively participate in the body of Christ and doesn't have friends who follow the Lord, he or she may never know what Christianity is really all about.

> As a huge fan of reality shows, I've noticed that Christians rarely come off looking good on network television. That's a shame, because it's not the Lord who behaves badly in those high-stress situations; it's the people who claim His name.

The only examples of Christ some folks will ever see are people who call themselves by His name. I'll be honest: It's not easy to maintain a Christian walk on a reality television program. These shows are based on high-pressure situations, and everyone is tense. Producers hope to capture tense, emotional moments in order to create an entertaining show that people—like me—will want to watch. It's easy to "slip" in such circumstances, and the ever-watchful eye of the camera does not forget—or forgive.

As I lived and worked in front of the *American Idol* cameras, I did so with the knowledge that I was representing far more than myself—I was representing my family, my friends, and the Lord.

What *Is* a Christian, Anyway?

In a country often defined as a "Christian nation," some people tend to assume that if you're American, you must be a Christian; if you celebrate Christmas, you're a Christian. If you're not Jewish, Muslim, or pagan, you're Christian by default. That's not really the case.

> As I lived and worked in front of the *American Idol* cameras, I did so with the knowledge that I was representing far more than myself—I was representing my family, my friends, and my Lord.

Others would give the easy answer and say, "Well, if you believe in Jesus, you're a Christian." That's not the case either.

A lot of people believe that Jesus was born some two thousand years ago, that He was a good man and a great teacher, and that He died on a cross. Some of those folks even believe He rose from the dead. Some of them also believe that heaven waits on the other side of death and if we are really good people, we'll meet Him at the pearly gates.

But the truth is, getting to heaven has nothing to do with good deeds—and everything to do with God's grace.

What is a Christian? The Word of God gives us the answer: "If you confess with your mouth that Jesus is Lord and believe in your heart that God raised him from the dead, you will be saved. For it is by believing in your heart that you are made right with God, and it is by confessing with your mouth that you are saved" (Romans 10:9-10).

Believing is a simple thing, so easy even a child can do it, but just as you can love your child one way and love french fries in another, there are different kinds of belief. The Latin language expresses these three different ideas beautifully.

The first word we translate "believe" is the Latin word *noticia*. This is an intellectual acknowledgment. Many people intellectually believe that Jesus lived and died, and they call themselves Christians.

The second word we translate "believe" is *assentia*. It involves assent, or agreement, and if you hold this sort of belief, you agree with a person's position or ideals. Saying "I believe in his cause" means you *agree* with it.

The third word we translate "believe" is *fiducia*. This is the word we find in Scripture; it's the Greek word *pisteuo. Fiducia* belief involves more than intellectual acknowledgment or agreement. This type of belief involves firm reliance, an entrusting of something to someone. When you *fiducia*-believe in someone or something, you are firmly trusting in it.

So, there are people who mentally acknowledge that Christ lived. There are others who agree with His principles, that love and meekness and kindness are good things. But there are others who have entrusted their lives to Jesus. They have turned over their right to call the shots, and they acknowledge Jesus Christ as Lord of their past, present, and future. They're not perfect people, but when they mess up, they admit their mistakes and ask the Lord to put them back in the center of His will.

Jesus explained it in the following story:

> A farmer went out to plant some seed. As he scattered it across his field, some of the seed fell on a footpath, and the birds came and ate it. Other seed fell on shallow soil with underlying rock. The seed sprouted quickly because the soil was shallow. But the plant soon wilted under the hot sun, and since it didn't have deep roots, it died. Other seed fell among thorns that

Even at two I loved chicken! (1978)

If you look past the dirty child in the front, you can see the ugliest couch in America in the back! (1980)

Happy Birthday! Mmm . . . cake!
(1982)

Half brother, Bryan; brother, John;
stepsister, Vonnie; and me on a family vacation.
I was not a happy camper!
(June 1988)

Mom and me. Mom was always around to take
me to my choir competitions and performances.
(February 1992)

Me in my drill team uniform
(1992)

Dad, John; Mom, Ruby; and me at my high school graduation. Note the Sara Lee cheesecake I'm clinging to, a graduation gift from someone who knew it was my favorite. (May 1994)

"Roomdawgs" forever! My college roommate, Pam, and me. (November 1997)

Dad and me after my final
Fisk Jubilee Singers concert
(May 2000)

Dad, John; Mom, Ruby; and me at
my graduation from Fisk University
(May 24, 2000)

Left to right: Sherry Carter, Angela Cottrell, Tammy Jensen, Chance Scoggins, and me after my first Living Proof Live event in Charlotte, North Carolina (July 2001)

Best friend, Chandra Bennett, and me (December 2003)

Travis Cottrell and Beth Moore after a Living Proof Live event (May 2002)

Travis Cottrell and me. This is a perfect depiction of how sweet and kind I am and how crazy Travis is! (February 2004)

Living Proof Live, Knoxville, Tennessee. Top row: Kevin Perry, Kevin Jones, Chance Scoggins, me, Angela Cruz. Bottom row: Chris Thom, Tammy Jensen, Beth Moore, Travis Cottrell, Angela Cottrell, Alexis Cruz. (September 2005)

One of the many
characters I met
in Chicago
(September 18, 2005)

Dorothy(?) and I wait for
our interviews in Chicago.
(September 18, 2005)

Derrell and Terrell Brittenum waiting to sing for Simon, Paula, and Randy (September 20, 2005)

Brother, John; me; stepsister, Vonnie; and half brother, Bryan, at Christmas in Georgia (December 2005)

Princess Mandisa at the premier party at Chance and Jennifer's house
(January 17, 2006)

Eagerly watching the show with my friends, including Angela Cruz, pictured in background (January 17, 2006)

Kevin and Alicia Perry dropped by after the show to enjoy the festivities and make sure I was okay. (January 17, 2006)

Me with Tammy Jensen and Chance Scoggins (January 17, 2006)

Chance and Jennifer Scoggins threw a great party and even made these T-shirts to support me! (January 17, 2006)

My stepmom, Millie; dad, John; and mom, Ruby, at the show during "Songs of the Twenty-First Century" week (March 28, 2006)

I had just made it through the executive-producer round and was greeted by a beaming Pam! (September 16, 2005)

Pam eagerly waited behind me to snap this picture after I made it past the first round in Chicago. (September 16, 2005)

Chandra was in the audience the night I made it to the top twelve. (March 9, 2006)

My mom, Ruby; me; and my brother, John, backstage at the American Idols Live concert in Sacramento (August 29, 2006)

grew up and choked out the tender plants so they produced no grain. Still other seeds fell on fertile soil, and they sprouted, grew, and produced a crop that was thirty, sixty, and even a hundred times as much as had been planted! (Mark 4:3-8)

Do you see what He was illustrating? The seed is the good news about Jesus, and some people don't receive it at all. Others learn about it and are excited for a while; then they burn out. Others agree with it and seem to accept it, but eventually the cares of life choke it out. Finally, there are those who receive the good news about Jesus deep in their hearts, and it changes their lives forever.

Jesus pointed out, "Not everyone who calls out to me, 'Lord! Lord!' will enter the Kingdom of Heaven. Only those who actually do the will of my Father in heaven will enter. On judgment day many will say to me, 'Lord! Lord! We prophesied in your name and cast out demons in your name and performed many miracles in your name.' But I will reply, 'I never knew you. Get away from me, you who break God's laws.'" (Matthew 7:21-23).

Here's the thing: I can't judge the condition of a person's heart. I don't know who's really godly and who's not, but God knows. Furthermore, those who truly follow the Lord and are filled with His Spirit bear the kind of fruit listed in Galatians 5:22-23: love, joy, peace, patience, kindness, goodness, faithfulness, gentleness, and self-control. When I see those qualities in a person's life, I have a good indication they're following Jesus.

During my time with *Idol*, I wanted people to see me as belonging to the group that received the fourth sprinkling of seeds—those who have received the Word and have it rooted deep in their hearts. Since the Spirit lives in me, I wanted His fruit to splash out of my life and onto the people I met at the show, as well as anyone who happened to be watching on TV.

> It's been estimated that thirty million people watch each episode of *American Idol.* The sheer size of that number still boggles my mind, but I saw *Idol* as an unprecedented opportunity to represent Jesus.

It's been estimated that thirty million people watch each episode of *American Idol.* The sheer size of that number still boggles my mind, but I saw *Idol* as an unprecedented opportunity to represent Jesus.

Measuring Motives

Since graduating from college, I had been living in a quiet and protected goldfish bowl. I worked for a Christian company, associated with Christian friends, sang with a Christian group. I loved being surrounded by other believers, because they taught and encouraged me, and the Lord used that time to fill my head and heart with lessons I would need in the days ahead.

I am thankful for my "goldfish bowl" experience, but I also recognize that God has called me to carry His name into the unpredictable roaring sea as well.

Shortly after my first audition aired, I received an e-mail from an acquaintance. She wrote, "I was not happy with your *American Idol* experience. You do not have to compromise your values and sing secular music to make money and a name for yourself. I just hate that we as the Christian community cannot pay you the same money as the secular, but the rewards are much greater."

After reading her message, I stared at the computer screen in shock. How could she possibly feel that way? If Christians associated only with other Christians, how would unbelievers come to know Jesus?

Suddenly I realized that this woman couldn't be the only one with these doubts about me. Many Christians believe we should remain separate from those who do not share our views and beliefs. They quote 2 Corinthians 6:17 as their rationale: "Come out from among unbelievers, and separate yourselves from them, says the LORD. Don't touch their filthy things, and I will welcome you."

But Paul meant that we should separate ourselves from the sinful practices of those who don't know God. We're not to participate in ungodly activities.

Furthermore, Jesus himself endured criticism for talking to fallen women, eating with tax collectors, and visiting sinners. He regularly told us that we should let our lights shine out to the world, not hide them under a bushel basket.

In His prayer at the Last Supper, Jesus talked to His heavenly Father about us:

> "I have given them your word. And the world hates them because they do not belong to the world, just as I do not belong to the world. I'm not asking you to take them out of the world, but to keep them safe from the evil one. They do not belong to this world any more than I do. Make them holy by your truth; teach them your word, which is truth. Just as you sent me into the world, I am sending them into the world." (John 17:14-18)

I sat for a long while and considered that e-mail, searching my heart to see if this might be God's way of pointing out some blind spot in my life. I wanted to be open to correction, and I know God often speaks through His people. If He did not want me to move on, I was not going to.

As I asked the Lord for guidance, He posed a question to me: *What is your motive?*

Was it as my acquaintance suggested? Was I doing this to make money and a name for myself? I shuddered at the thought. Although money and fame have never been my goal, I couldn't help but recognize that I'd been granted an opportunity to represent Jesus through the gifts He had given me. I sought His glory over my own success.

I immediately felt the peace of God, so I responded to my acquaintance's e-mail, thanked her for sharing her concern, and assured her that I had pure motives. I was grateful for her letter because it made me stop and evaluate my intentions; then it strengthened my intention to maintain a strong testimony before the other contestants and the staff of *American Idol*.

Shortly after making it into the top twenty-four, I sent an e-mail to a group of friends who had promised to pray for me. I suggested that if anyone mentioned the show, why not turn the occasion into an opportunity for ministry? For instance, they could say something like, "Mandisa just sent out an e-mail and said if anyone asked us about her, we should let you know that Jesus is the most important person in her life. I was just wondering—do you have a relationship with Him?"

A lot of people wrote to tell me they had done that. One woman said that for months she had been trying to talk about Christianity to a coworker who hadn't been interested in pursuing the conversation. But after an episode of *Idol*, the woman approached her and said, "That Mandisa—she's a Christian, isn't she?"

My friend said, "Yes, she is."

"Interesting," the coworker replied. "She's a lot different from what I've seen in the past."

Wow—an open door for my friend to speak to her coworker about Jesus.

My desire to share Jesus with others stems from the joy, purpose, and validation He has brought into my life. Out of love for others I want them to experience that same joy, purpose, and validation, which comes only from a relationship with Jesus. I also want them to know, beyond a shadow of a doubt, that if they were to die tonight, they would go to heaven. Asking Jesus into my heart and life was the best decision I ever made. I want to help others make the same decision.

Over the months following the show, I have heard from many people who were moved by my response to Simon, by my testimony, and by other events that unfolded as the show progressed.

I am grateful for those contacts, and I know one thing: I don't think I could have made it through the *Idol* experience without the faithful prayers of God's people. I wrote my prayer intercessors every week, and I know some of those e-mails were forwarded to other believers around the world. I felt the power of those prayers, especially as the competition advanced.

I didn't realize how soon I would need the power of those prayers.

7 Joy and Gladness

After we found out who was in the top twenty-four, the show officials sent us home to spend the next two weeks preparing for the semifinals and the finals, the most demanding part of the *American Idol* competition. We were to return to Los Angeles on February 10, and we had to be prepared to stay until May 25. Now, more than ever before, we became almost painfully aware that we weren't involved in a mere contest; we were involved in a television production . . . and a top-rated production at that.

Ryan Seacrest announced the twenty-four remaining contestants on February 15, 2006. Twelve male singers and twelve female singers would compete, with two men and two women being eliminated each week. The semifinals would last for three weeks, with three prime-time shows airing per week. The pace quickened dramatically, and from the time I crawled out of bed each morning until the time I slipped back between the sheets at night, I barely had time to catch my breath.

The pace was easier to manage than my first Hollywood week, however, because between my Chicago audition and the time I went back in February, I had lost thirty pounds by working out several hours a day and staying away from fast foods and sweets. It paid off, because people noticed. Furthermore, they kept noticing, and it was a little disconcerting to realize that I had been called to live out my battle with food addiction in front of everyone. Every time I sat down to eat, I felt as if people looked at my plate and did a mental calorie count: *Is she being good? Should she be eating that potato?*

Maybe I was being paranoid, but I considered my new commitment to healthy eating as much a part of my challenge as the music was. I was not aiming to "get skinny"—I've always wanted to "get healthy." To anyone who asked, I said you don't have to be a size two to be an American Idol. Beauty comes in all shapes and sizes.

After arriving in Hollywood, we were housed in a swanky hotel in Beverly Hills. I had been praying that the Lord would prepare me for whoever my roommate would be, and I'd been considering the possibilities. Of the twelve female finalists, three

> I had been called to live out my battle with food addiction in front of everyone.

> I was not aiming to "get skinny"—I've always wanted to "get healthy." To anyone who asked, I said you don't have to be a size two to be an American Idol. Beauty comes in all shapes and sizes.

were minors and had to stay with a chaperone. The remaining nine women would have to pair up in rooms. If the producers followed the routine they had established during Hollywood week, they would group us according to age.

As the oldest contestant, I thought I might be fortunate enough to snag a room to myself—I'm an introvert, remember? I was begging God to make my wish a reality and reminded Him I needed time alone because it's hard to focus on prayer with a stranger in the room.

If that weren't enough, I also reminded the Lord about my strange habits. I can't fall asleep without my sleep machine, which I program to chirp with frog song, the babble of a brook, or a rushing wind that absolutely *must* continue through the night. If the power goes off and the machine stops, I wake up—and that's not a good thing when you're running on adrenaline in your waking hours.

When I *do* get up, I like to run through my vocal exercises, which is not always a welcome sound early in the morning. I should take this opportunity to apologize to my former roommates for the *geh, geh, gehs* and the *nee, nee, nees* that must have slapped them from sleep as I sang in the shower.

So, mostly out of love and concern for my fellow contestants, I begged the Lord for my own space. I was delighted when I got to my room, pulled the key card out of the door, and entered to find one king-size bed instead of two queens! The Lord was smiling down on me.

The media rep had filled our first week with press interviews, so I pulled new clothes from my suitcase and slipped into them, grateful that I looked nice. At this point we were still responsible for our own wardrobe, hair, and makeup. I was thrilled because I had just come from a Beth Moore event in

New York City, where I had discovered a plus-size clothing store called Ashley Stewart.

I went crazy in that store! They offered cute, urban-influenced, plus-sized clothes at a great price. In the dressing room my excitement ratcheted up a level when I discovered I had dropped a couple of sizes. I don't always enjoy shopping for new clothes, but that was one of the best shopping experiences of my life. Even big girls want to look good, and I haven't found more than a handful of stores that understand how someone like me wants to look. Granted, I won't wear a halter top or a short skirt, but I do look for clothes that flatter my curvy shape. No floral patterns or muumuus for me! Ashley Stewart got that. Ashley Stewart, whoever she was, was my new best friend.

Feeling especially cute, I went upstairs to join the others for the interview sessions. The Fox publicists had rented a large conference room on the top floor of our hotel. Representatives from media outlets across the country came to find out more about the *Idol* top twenty-four. The vestibule outside the conference room was a den of nervous chatter as we contestants awaited our debut into pop culture. The caterers had set up a table of light breakfast foods, and the room smelled of pineapple and pastries. Large windows overlooked the stunning Beverly Hills skyline. Although clouds blocked the sun, the eighty-degree day was a vast improvement over the forty-degree weather I had left in Nashville.

I munched on watermelon, grapes, and fresh pineapple slices and quietly observed the people around me. Some of the guys stepped outside to the balcony to have a smoke, but most of the girls stayed inside to dish on wardrobe and makeup secrets.

I should have felt confident, right? There I was, a daughter of the King, in new clothes, in a new size, and thirty pounds lighter on my feet. I had made it to the top twenty-four, and soon I would be singing for America.

Confident? Let me tell you: I felt *intimidated* as I looked around at the other women. Every last one of them was gorgeous. From Kellie Pickler, a beautiful blonde, to Becky O'Donahue, a striking green-eyed brunette, I knew I'd be facing an impossible challenge if I tried to measure up to them physically.

I flashed back to my first day of sixth grade. The way I saw it back then, reaching the sixth grade meant I was practically an adult. When we went back-to-school shopping, I asked my mom if I could pick out some things rather than let her choose everything. She agreed, so I was giddy with anticipation when we walked into the children's department of Mervyn's.

Mom picked out the usual outfits, adorned with flower prints and happy faces, but I was looking for something much cooler. I finally spotted it around the corner: a pink and black striped button down shirt with a hot pink T-shirt underneath (it was the eighties). My mom grimaced as I walked up holding my hip new outfit, but she relented, and I walked out of the store ready to face the sixth grade.

On Monday morning, as I climbed the steps of Mariposa Elementary School, I knew someone simply *had* to notice how cool I looked, but no one said a thing about my new shirt. I went home feeling disappointed and wondered if my new outfit was really as great as I had thought it was.

Now, as I sat in my new clothes with the other eleven girls, I wondered the same thing. Eventually I shook off the feeling and decided I wasn't going to compare myself with anyone else. I was going to be the best Mandisa I could be and leave the rest in the hands of America—and God, who would certainly take care of me.

After another short speech about what to expect that day, we were paired with one other contestant to make our rounds. Kat and I were assigned to be partners, and we were the first to enter the conference room. As those double doors swung open, I froze. The room was brimming with lights and cameras and men and women dressed in business suits and carrying microphones. Each media rep had been assigned an area, and the areas were designated by partitions and signs on the floor.

I felt a shiver snake up my spine. For the first time in my life, I was experiencing a small measure of fame— and I wasn't sure I wanted it.

> For the first time in my life, I was experiencing a small measure of fame, and I wasn't sure I wanted it.

That's when I began to realize that people are genuinely hungry for information about people who are on television. This insatiable need to know doesn't make much sense, but the reporters were quick to jot down anything we were willing to tell them, and sometimes they were interested in the craziest details.

In an interview for the last semifinal show, I mentioned a strange-but-true fact: I had sucked my thumb until I was twenty-four years old. (It's a miracle my teeth don't stretch from here to Budapest!)

But one day I read Mary Hunt's *The Financially Confident Woman*. Hunt said you could change a habit by making a concerted effort for twenty-one days, so taking her at her word, I decided not to suck my thumb for twenty-one days, and I broke the habit. Accomplishing that small goal helped me see that I can meet my weight-loss goals, too; it's all a matter of setting my mind and will to doing or not doing something for a set number of days.

As Kat and I moved from station to station, we found that whether we were being interviewed by the Fox affiliate in Fresno or in New York, the reporters asked the same questions: Why should you be the next American Idol? Vocally, to whom can you compare yourself? Who is your favorite judge? What is your strangest habit?

By the end of that long day I was more than ready to turn on my noise machine and hit the sack.

The next day we sat through more press interviews, this time for national entertainment shows: *Extra, Entertainment Tonight, The Insider, Access Hollywood,* and many more. I enjoyed the attention, but I couldn't help thinking it odd that almost overnight I'd gone from being a regular girl to being a hot media personality. After all, *I* hadn't changed. Only my circumstances had.

After two days of meeting the press, we finally got down to the reason we'd come together—to sing.

Before we arrived in California, we had been asked to submit a list of six songs we wanted to perform on the show. I had chosen my songs carefully. First, I would not sing anything that did not align with my value system. If I was going to represent a holy God, I could not sing songs about bumping and grinding!

Second, I wanted to sing songs that would stretch people's view of me. Since "soul" songs come most naturally for me, I would hold off on Aretha Franklin, Whitney Houston, and Chaka Khan tunes for the first couple of weeks.

Finally, with only one and a half minutes to impress America, I would have to pick songs that highlighted the best parts of my voice. With these criteria in mind, I found six songs that fit the bill.

As we rushed through the whirlwind of press interviews, a department within the production company was busy contacting publishers to get permission to use these songs on the show. When they had finished, we were each handed a manila envelope containing sheet music for the songs that had cleared copyrights and permissions.

For my first performance I chose the Heart tune "Never," because I knew people wouldn't expect a rock song from me. I wanted to rise above the pack.

The song helped me do just that. When our first show aired on February 21, the producers selected me to open the show. Still responsible for my own clothes, hair, and makeup, I wore a red bustier with a sheer black top over it. I'd ironed my hair bone-straight and topped off my look with bright red lipstick. I burst onto the stage feeling confident and original. The judges and America agreed with my assessment as I sailed into the top twenty.

I was on my way.

Extra Grace Required

Although back at the hotel I was enjoying the large room I had all to myself, I knew I'd eventually have to share a room. The Lord had been good to give me time alone, and I wanted Him to continue to work in the room assignments.

As people began to be eliminated and go home, I wasn't sure whether or not the room assignments would still be determined by age. If so, the next closest to me in age was Kinnik Sky, and we'd grown close since our arrival in Hollywood. Like me, Kinnik loved the Lord, and I enjoyed her company.

On the other hand, if the Lord wanted to stretch my ability to be gracious, He might put me with a certain other contestant, whose name I'm not going to mention. What can I say about this young woman? She's someone I usually refer to as an EGR—meaning Extra Grace Required.

From the beginning she had made it clear that she hadn't come to California to make friends. She was there to win.

In my daily prayer time I began to understand that I was supposed to pray for this girl. So I prayed and looked for opportunities to love her.

One day I noticed that she was upset about something, so I wrote her a note and said I'd be there for her if she ever wanted to talk. Whenever I heard other people say negative things about her, I tried to point out that we really didn't know her background or circumstances and maybe there were valid reasons for her attitude.

Despite my initial dislike, I began to be intrigued by this young woman and felt called to offer her unconditional love.

Well. Hear me when I say that it's easy to tell the Lord you'll love someone unconditionally when you're sleeping in another room. When her roommate was eliminated, I saw the writing on the wall and *knew* what the Lord had in mind. I begged Him to change His plans. Surely He couldn't expect me to love someone while sharing the same bathroom!

Right after I told the Lord what He should do next, He led me to open a book of collected Scripture verses. I chuckled as I read the passage for the day: "Should we accept only good things from the hand of God and never anything bad?" (Job 2:10); "I know, O Lord, that your regulations are fair; you disciplined me because I needed it" (Psalm 119:75); "It is the Lord's will. . . . Let him do what he thinks best" (1 Samuel 3:18).

The Lord made it pretty clear that He had a purpose for what He was about to do.

I had just relented and agreed to abide by His will when my phone rang with the official news. I was to pack my belongings and move next door—with my extra-grace-required girl.

When I began to carry my things into the room, I discovered that my new roommate wasn't home. I slipped out to visit Kinnik and ask for her prayers. She immediately joined me in praying over that room. What a sight we must have been as we covered room 309 with prayer!

As I prayed for my new roomie, I felt the Lord telling me that my time with this lonely girl would be short because she would be eliminated that week. I also thought the Lord was telling me that I would make it into the top three.

So, after hearing what I believed was the Lord's assurance that my time with my new roommate would be limited, I decided to make the most of my days with her. When she came in later that night, I was already snuggled in my bed. I planned to rise early because I was going to church in L.A. with some of the other girls. I invited her to join us, but she passed.

The next morning, Kellie, Kinnik, and I boarded our black Ford Explorer with our bodyguard, Rydell (whose first experience with church had taken place in season four with Bo Bice; his second time was with us), and we drove to Saddleback Church in Lake Forest. The previous November I had sung at a conference in Orlando with Saddleback's pastor, Rick Warren, so I called my friend Tim, one of the worship leaders at Saddleback, to see if he'd be in town on our Sunday off. We'd like to attend their church, I explained, and I wanted to see him but wanted to be sure I didn't miss him in that huge crowd.

Tim not only made sure I didn't miss him; he also treated us like royalty! As we entered the parking lot of the megachurch, we felt as if we were in a presidential motorcade. We hadn't asked for special attention, but ushers were waiting to escort us to Pastor Warren's office. Gracious as always, he spent a few moments with us and gave us each a signed copy of *The Purpose Driven Life.*

That was honor enough, but next they ushered us into the main sanctuary, where Pastor Rick welcomed us onto the platform so we could greet the church members. The audience erupted into applause as the three of us walked up the stairs.

The worship leader exhorted the audience to use the gifts that God had given them to be a light. He commended us for doing just that, and the choir began to sing as we walked off the stage.

The three of us settled into our seats for an amazing time of worshipping and studying God's Word. That hour was just what we needed, and we left that body of believers feeling refreshed and excited about what God was doing in our lives.

Back at the hotel I was beginning to enjoy my time with my new roommate. She taught me how to hem a blouse, shared some of her dreams, and even commented that she thought I was one of the few "real" people in the competition. We had a serious conversation about God, and to this day I continue to keep her in my prayers.

In the competition that week, I maintained my strategy of presenting the unexpected by singing a country song, Faith Hill's "Cry." I wanted a more classic look for this performance, so I wore a flowing black and silver outfit and put my hair up in a bun. Randy didn't like the song choice, but said he really wanted me to do my thing.

Paula liked the song and recognized that I was taking different kinds of songs and making them my own. She also added that I had a beautiful face.

I was so grateful for her encouragement. When you're standing on that stage before the judges and the TV cameras, you feel a bit like a puppy stranded on the highway with an 18-wheeler bearing down on you.

I braced for the semi named Simon. He confessed he preferred the look I'd worn the previous week and said he didn't care for the song, but he summed up his critique by saying, "When you're at your best, there's not a female competitor who can beat you." He predicted that America would keep me around for another week. He was right.

When my new roommate was eliminated that week, I placed a checkmark next to the things I'd written in my journal:

- The Lord had told me I'd move in with my EGR. *Check.*
- The Lord had told me she would be eliminated that week. *Check.*
- The Lord had told me I would make it to the top three. No check yet, but maybe soon.

Because the Lord had spoken so clearly about the first two things, I believed He'd keep His third promise to me. I would be staying in California several more weeks.

A Welcome Respite

The Lord blessed me when Kinnik moved in next. Aside from her wanting the thermostat set at eighty-five and her attachment to a crazy blue night light, I enjoyed spending time with her.

I knew I had to lay it all on the line during the last week of the semifinals. The time had come for me to do my music my way. The easy choice for me was Chaka Khan's "I'm Every Woman." The lyrics were easy for me to relate to, and the soaring notes highlighted the best part of my voice.

I hoped this would be the night that ensured my spot in the elite top twelve. Everyone focused on this goal, because the top twelve contestants moved to a bigger stage with a larger audience. The stakes increased with every passing day, but I was feeling up to the challenge.

On March 7, I bounced onto the stage feeling comfortable in my jeans and brown top. With gold boots on my feet and my hair dangling on my shoulders, I swept across the stage proclaiming that I *was* every woman! The words of the bridge came out of my mouth with emphatic crispness:

> *I ain't braggin',*
> *'cause I'm the one.*
> *Just ask me and it shall be done.*
> *Don't bother to compare, 'cause I got it!*

I sang those words as if claiming them for myself. I felt I'd hit the mark when Randy and Paula gave me a standing ovation and Simon said I was in a different league from the other girls, predicting that I would sail into the top twelve.

My elation, however, was dampened by my concern for Kinnik. While I considered my new roomie an enormous talent, as I prayed for whoever would be eliminated the next morning, my mind kept turning to her. I begged the Lord to assure me that this feeling was wrong, but the sense of foreboding persisted.

On March 9, we gathered to hear the names of the top twelve contestants. I sat on the risers with the remaining seven ladies and waited for Ryan to announce the results.

"Mandisa," he read in his disc jockey voice, "you sang 'I'm Every Woman.'" He continued by reading the judges' comments. Then he glanced at me and smiled. "Earlier in the season Simon asked if we had a bigger stage for you—"

Thanks for that reminder, Ryan.

"Well, we do. You're in the top twelve!"

I sighed in relief as I strolled off of the stage and sat on another itty-bitty stool. I stayed on that uncomfortable seat and tried to ignore the creeping numbness in my rear as I listened to Ryan announce the bottom three, composed that week of Ayla Brown, Melissa McGhee, and Kinnik. Two of them would be going home while the other took the last seat in the final twelve.

"The person with the lowest number of votes," Ryan said, "is Kinnik."

Tears welled in my eyes as I absorbed the sad news. I had also grown close to Ayla, who, for a seventeen-year-old, was as beautiful, talented, and intelligent as a girl can be.

Though I was happy for Melissa and her advancement, in that moment the harsh reality of this competition hit me with fresh force. As our group became smaller, the remaining contestants grew closer. And as we grew closer, the farewells would become more difficult.

> As our group became smaller, the remaining contestants grew closer. And as we grew closer, the farewells would become more difficult.

The cruel nature of the beast.

After the show I took a minute to catch my breath, a little surprised by the revelation: I had made it into the top twelve! Another goal accomplished. Next goal: cracking the top ten.

But first, we had to party! Ace, Bucky, Chris, Elliott, Katharine, Kellie, Kevin, Lisa, Melissa, Paris, Taylor, and I were whisked off to a local club for our top-twelve reveal. As we stepped out of our Ford Explorer, we were blinded by camera flashes and overwhelmed with photographers yelling our names so we'd look at them for a good shot. We worked the red carpet for an hour, doing on-the-spot interviews for TV, radio, newspapers, and magazines.

I have to admit, hearing my name on those reporters' lips was fun and exciting. After all, only a few weeks before, no one in Hollywood had ever heard my name—and certainly couldn't have pronounced it.

But it didn't take long for me to realize that fame is a double-edged sword. Fame giveth, but she also taketh away.

Celebrity—A Blessing and a Responsibility

The bright light of celebrity began to shine on us in earnest at that point. Being "famous" gives me a platform to talk about things some people are reluctant to mention, including faith and food issues. In addition, I had the testimony of Scripture to support my willingness to embrace a measure of celebrity. It's true that God honors the humble, but He also lifts people to positions of prominence for His purposes. Joseph was raised from a prison pit to the second-highest throne in Egypt. Daniel, held captive in Babylon, became chief of all the wise men and acted as a trusted counselor to several kings. Esther, an orphaned Jewish girl, became queen of Persia, and the list goes on. God can—and sometimes does—put His people in high places. I just had to be sure I didn't start taking credit for what was God's doing.

I have to be honest, though. I'm not always comfortable working a crowd, and sometimes I'd like to be able to go out without being recognized. Even now, months after the *Idol* competition, people routinely recognize me in restaurants and other public places.

Even in my small measure of fame, however, I see the Lord working to keep me humble. On several occasions, after being recognized as the girl on *American Idol,* I've been asked, "So, how is that movie going with Beyoncé?"

Wrong Idol, wrong season. While I love being compared to the fabulous Jennifer Hudson, we really don't look alike. When I lose a hundred pounds, maybe the resemblance will be a little greater.

In any case, I always try to smile and be pleasant when people come up to meet me, but like anyone else, I have insecurities, and they rear their gnarly little heads whenever I see people pointing and whispering.

Even among my closest friends I tend to be a private person. So being in the public eye was quite an adjustment.

A free tip for all future *American Idol* contestants: Make sure your phone number cannot be found on the Internet.

My Chicago audition aired on Tuesday, January 17. It was fun to be recognized by the police officer who pulled me over in Chance's neighborhood, but it wasn't fun to wake up on Wednesday morning and find forty-eight missed calls on my telephone. (A free tip for all future *American Idol* contestants: Make sure your phone number cannot be found on the Internet.)

I sat up in bed and rubbed my eyes to be sure I was seeing correctly. I thought maybe my phone had wigged out and gone ballistic. To confirm, I dialed my voice mail and heard the electronic woman inform me that I had thirty-seven new messages. It would take all morning to listen to all of them, but I was intrigued.

Message number one came in at 3:30 a.m. (When *do* people sleep?) and was from the Chuck and Jim Morning Show somewhere in New York. With all the pep they could muster, Chuck and Jim asked me to return their call so they could interview me on the air.

Messages two through thirty-seven were messages of congratulations from old friends from high school and college, or from radio, television, magazine, or newspaper reporters requesting interviews.

Overwhelmed, I replaced the receiver on the hook and sat in silence to catch my breath. What had I gotten myself into? I finally felt like the most popular girl in school, but the feeling wasn't as exhilarating as I'd thought it would be. While the positive comments made me feel great, another part of me felt invaded.

I picked up the phone and called BellSouth to change my phone number.

A couple of weeks later I checked my apartment mailbox and was surprised to find three letters from fans requesting my autograph. Happy to please, I responded with a signed head shot and a warm letter of thanks. I was sure those letters were flukes, but then my mailbox flooded with similar requests. I couldn't keep up!

Phone calls and fan letters are usually innocent, but what happened one night frightened me. At ten o'clock, I was home alone and wearing the purple sweat suit I like to sleep in. I had applied a white Proactiv facial mask, wrapped my hair up in a scarf, and snuggled under a blanket on my couch to watch an episode of *Extreme Makeover: Home Edition*.

Then I heard a knock at my front door. I paused my TiVo and crept to the foyer, wondering who in the world would be visiting at this time of night. My peephole revealed two strangers wearing baseball hats and holding beer bottles. As I squinted out, trying to remember whether or not I'd seen these men before, one of them yelled, "We know you're in there, Miss Idol. Your light is on, and we heard your TV."

I stepped back and gasped—a sound they probably heard. What was I supposed to do about *this*? Were they drunk? Should I call the police?

I inched forward again and peered out as the two men continued to wait by my door. They made light conversation with each other, smiling and waving and laughing as if it were no big deal to call on a stranger at night.

On the other side of the door, I was having a panic attack and wishing I had a big dog—or even a *tape* of a big, growly, hyperprotective rottweiler.

After another minute, the two men finally gave up and left. I turned off all the lights and the TV. Ty Pennington would have to wait.

Numb and weak-kneed, I sank to the sofa in complete darkness and contemplated my next move. As I sat, my heart slowly resumed its normal rhythm, and I prayed that this would be an isolated event. Changing apartments is far more complicated than changing a phone number.

I was suddenly eager to return to California and be with my friends from *Idol*. Sometimes that world felt more real and far safer than my apartment in Nashville.

8 Poor and Needy

With only twelve contestants left in season five, speculation began to run wild about who would eventually win. Six girls were competing against six guys, and I knew I was headed for the challenge of a lifetime.

Several magazines published articles predicting the eventual winner. One magazine praised me to the skies and said my rendition of "I'm Every Woman" had turned the production into a "one-woman show." Another magazine predicted that Taylor Hicks and I would be the final two.

Taylor had caught everyone's attention during Hollywood week. The first time I saw him walk onto the stage, I thought someone had made a mistake. This gray-haired guy had to be someone's father joking around. Then he began to sing, and I stared in awe as his voice took me back to the days when I used to listen to Michael McDonald and Ray Charles. My awe turned into wonder as he began to gyrate all over the stage. The man definitely had a gift for entertainment.

During the next break I called my friend and fellow *Idol* devotee Travis Cottrell. I told Travis I'd just seen the next winner. Travis listened as I went on and on about how incredible Taylor was. I knew he was definitely someone to watch.

Chris Daughtry also caught my eye, because he had several things going for him. First, he had what I considered the perfect combination–a bald head and a goatee. Chris was also one of the few married contestants, and he had children, which meant he and his family could be a rich vein of human interest features for the show. This "Rocker Dad" had all the makings of a superstar, and his incredible voice would be a natural fit for contemporary rock music. In early March, several magazines predicted that Chris and I would be the final two.

Other articles hailed Katharine, Paris, and Ace as the eventual winners. I tried not to pay too much attention to these predictions, because everyone had an opinion and no one could accurately predict how America would vote. I had to admit, though, it felt good to be affirmed as we entered the most grueling part of the competition.

Each of the remaining weeks would have a theme, and each week another contestant would be voted out of the contest. The competition would continue to get tougher—and not because of the judges, either. It was beginning to feel as if all of America were evaluat-

> Sometimes I wanted to be a fly on the wall behind a few company watercoolers after one of the final shows aired. I'm sure I would have heard some interesting conversations!

ing us. Sometimes I wanted to be a fly on the wall behind a few company watercoolers after one of the final shows aired. I'm sure I would have heard some interesting conversations!

We top twelve contestants were moved from our Beverly Hills hotel into apartments in the heart of Hollywood. Each apartment had two bedrooms, and each bedroom had two beds. I shared a room with Melissa, and across the hall, Katharine and Kellie roomed together and completed our cozy little home.

With the eleven other semifinalists, I settled down to work hard and do my best. I prayed about what God wanted me to do with this incredible opportunity—did He want me to *win* this contest? Did He want me to lose with grace? What, exactly, was His purpose in bringing me here?

One of the nice perks of the final round is the wardrobe stylist and hair/makeup team we were given to help with our presentation. Each week staffers gave us a budget and allowed us to pick out two complete outfits: one to wear for the performance and one to wear on the results show. Between rehearsals, we went shopping with our stylist to pick out our outfits.

For the first week, my stylist and I decided on a Spanish-inspired black skirt accented by red jewelry and a rose in my hair. My hairstylist, Teena, had done such beautiful things the previous year with Vonzell Solomon, so I felt completely at ease with her in charge of my look. I was used to doing my own makeup, but I yielded to the expert when I saw what Amy, my makeup artist, did with my face. I didn't know I could look that good!

We kicked off the finals by singing the songs of legendary artist Stevie Wonder. Earlier in the week we had met and performed our songs for Mr. Wonder. I was as nervous as a mouse as I stood before that living legend and performed "Don't

You Worry 'Bout a Thing." I couldn't have been more relieved and elated when he smiled and said I could sing just about anything.

One of the things I most remember about my first week in the top twelve was pain—from my shoes. I loved the stylists that worked with us on the show—after all, what woman doesn't love new clothes? But the shoes I was given to wear that first week made my "dogs" bark!

I remember sitting next to Ryan right before I took center stage to perform my Stevie Wonder classic. I wanted to do a good job, but my feet were throbbing so badly, I could barely even think about singing. Those spiked-heeled black and silver sandals looked good, but trust me, they weren't designed for walking.

Ryan looked at me and smiled. "How are you feeling, Mandisa?"

I gave him the honest truth: "My feet are killing me."

As I stared in disbelief, Ryan knelt down on the stage and unstrapped my sandals. Sing in my bare feet? Well, why not?

I grinned at Ryan and took him up on his unspoken challenge. I padded onto the stage in my bare feet and sang my heart out. The judges loved my song, and later, after the judges' comments, Ryan threw one of my shoes at Simon.

I think a lot of women felt liberated by my barefoot performance. I wished I could go shoeless more often.

The judges must have felt my joy, as did America, because they voted me into the top eleven.

Unfortunately, my roommate, Melissa, was sent home that night, and I was beginning to be concerned because my fellow contestants were calling me the black widow. It was bad enough during Hollywood week, when *all* my roommates were sent home. But after making the top twenty-four, it was a little creepy when my first three roommates went home right after moving in with me. I began to wonder whether something was up.

I prayed about it and wrote the following in my journal: *Is this just a coincidence, Lord? Or is this part of Your plan? Could You have put me*

> My fellow contestants were calling me "the black widow."

with these people to be a comfort of sorts? To speak life before things get hard for them?

After praying about it, I decided the Lord had to be strategically placing me in situations where I could be a blessing to someone who needed to hear from Him. I thanked Him for the opportunity to minister to my past roommates and wondered if my "kiss of death" applied only to people actually in the room with me or if Kat and Kellie now stood in danger of elimination too.

Meeting with Manilow

The next week featured songs from the fifties. I was thrilled when we boarded a plane to Las Vegas to enlist the help of musical veteran Barry Manilow. I performed my version of Dinah Washington's "I Don't Hurt Anymore" and saw Mr. Manilow's brows rise as I reached for the big ending he had created for me.

When I had finished, Mr. Manilow said I could come and work for him if this *Idol* thing didn't work out. He marveled at my range and called me "one of a kind."

I felt honored that a veteran of the music industry was impressed with my effort. On March 21, the judges were impressed as well and responded with glowing remarks. Randy said my song was a classy and amazing way to start the show.

Paula called my performance "flawless." But Simon made my night when he announced that he *loved* it!

Taking his cue from a sign my friend Travis was holding in the audience, Ryan proclaimed that "*Mandiva* had arrived!"

I was humbled and grateful that America believed in me enough to vote me through to the top ten.

"Top ten" was more than a number to us contestants, because no matter who won, the top ten would reunite to travel on the American Idols Live summer tour. In previous seasons, nearly all top-ten contestants had been considered by major recording companies, so we were eager to reach that enviable position.

On March 22, we learned that Kevin "Chicken Little" Covais missed the top ten by one spot. I was truly sorry to see him go because I loved Kevin. The sixteen-year-old made us all laugh, and he always had some surprise up his sleeve. One night I caught him reciting every word of a Kanye West song. I never dreamed Kevin could rap!

The day before Kevin was eliminated, I had written this in my journal: *I feel very drawn to Kevin these days and hope to witness to him today or tomorrow before the results are announced. Order my steps, Lord.*

The day before the announcement, I also sent an e-mail to my intercessors, asking them to pray for me and for Kevin. I did speak to Kevin that day, and I continue to have a relationship with him. I think he is a special young man, and I believe the Lord has gifted him for great things.

Songs from the Twenty-First Century

As the next week approached, I couldn't help but be excited that we would be singing songs from the twenty-first century.

I kept thinking of Esther, the devout Jewish girl who'd been snatched up and placed in a pagan king's harem. (It's not that *American Idol* is anything like a harem, but there were several occasions when I felt about as out of place.)

When Esther faced a moral dilemma in the king's court, her uncle Mordecai sent her a message: "Who knows if perhaps you were made queen for just such a time as this?" (Esther 4:14).

So I sent an e-mail to my intercessors and asked them to forward it to other Christians who would pray for me. I knew I had reached a turning point, and I couldn't begin this next part of the journey without the Lord's help. I asked for prayer for myself, the judges, and the audience. I wanted each one of them to experience God in a way they never had before.

> "Who knows if perhaps you were made queen for just such a time as this?" (Esther 4:14).

In the e-mail, I couldn't reveal what I would be singing because producers had just met with us and told us that word had been getting out about who would be singing what each week.

After much prayer and godly counsel, I decided I would sing one of my favorites, Mary Mary's "Shackles (Praise You)" on March 28. The song, which I had sung so many times with my friends on the worship team, is a bold expression of the liberating power of God's grace.

I knew I couldn't attempt such a presentation relying on my own strength. When I had finished, I didn't want to hear "great job"; I wanted lives to be changed.

I told myself, "You don't have what you want because you don't ask God for it" (James 4:2). So I asked everyone I knew to pray for me. I was trusting God to do something incredible with that song. But before He could, I had to leap over a couple of hurdles the enemy placed in my way.

I'm convinced that during the competition God kept His hand on me not only emotionally and spiritually but also physically. *American Idol* is physically and mentally grueling because we are continually exercising a fragile muscle—the voice—and we don't always get enough sleep. I tried to stay healthy by exercising, eating right, and loading up on vitamins, but during that next week my roommates, Katharine and Kellie, came down with highly contagious strep throat. Even though they were moved out of the apartment and quarantined, their germs stayed behind. I was terrified I'd get strep, but instead I caught something else—a type of staphylococcus. While Kat and Kellie recovered from their illness, I got sick and had to sing through it, even though my throat felt thick and swollen. My infection wasn't severe because I caught it early. The moment I started feeling bad, I saw the doctor and got some antibiotics.

> *American Idol* is physically and mentally grueling because we are continually exercising a fragile muscle—the voice—and we don't always get enough sleep.

That entire week I had to rehearse and sing through the lethargy that accompanies a slight fever. But you know what they say in Hollywood: The show must go on.

So it did.

Shackles

I had carefully planned and prayed for every detail of the night that I was to sing "Shackles." Believers all across America had joined me in fasting and prayer. I wanted this to be a night when the Spirit of God reigned, but unknown to me, the evil one had upset my plans and was about to steal my peace of mind.

For that night I had planned to wear a red football jersey with the words *Galatians 5:1* emblazoned on the front. However, just minutes before I was to take the stage, I was told that I would not be able to wear it. I was really caught off guard and was terribly upset. Two steps from the stage, I said a quick prayer and begged God to focus my mind and heal my broken heart and throbbing throat.

Then the music began.

As I walked down the ramp to center stage, I lifted my chin and proclaimed, "This song goes out to everybody who wants to be free. Your addiction, lifestyle, or situation may be big, but God is bigger."

Then, empowered by a surge of strength from on high, I sang my song. By the time the last beat hit, I felt *great*. The audience sprang to their feet, and I was pretty sure even the angels were applauding in victory. The evil one had tried to foil our plans, but God wouldn't let him. I deflected the applause that came my way by lifting my hands in applause to the true King.

As I walked down the ramp to center stage, I lifted my chin and proclaimed, "This song goes out to everybody who wants to be free. Your addiction, lifestyle, or situation may be big, but God is bigger."

Looking out across the cheering crowd, I saw my mom, dad, stepmom, and my roomdawg, Pam, in the audience. They knew the significance of what had just happened. They got it.

The judges, however, didn't understand. While Randy admitted I was one of the best singers in the competition, he ended by saying, "I don't quite get it." Paula, as kind as ever, said, "All I know is there's a new religion and forty million people have now joined the church of Mandisa."

I appreciated the compliment in her words, but I cringed at the thought of glory coming in my direction. The glory belonged only to Jesus.

Simon drove right to the point, abruptly saying that my song was "indulgent" and concluding that he "just didn't get that. Not for me."

The judges' words, while brief, spoke volumes about the difference between believers and unbelievers: "People who aren't spiritual can't receive these truths from God's Spirit. It all sounds foolish to them and they can't understand it, for only those who are spiritual can understand what the Spirit means. Those who are spiritual can evaluate all things, but they themselves cannot be evaluated by others" (1 Corinthians 2:14-15).

> Not until later did I learn that my five-second introduction to "Shackles" ignited a public firestorm.

Not until later did I learn that my five-second introduction to "Shackles" had ignited a public firestorm. When I mentioned addictions, lifestyles, and situations, I was referring to my struggle with food and my need for a lifestyle change. Not for one minute did I consider that the word *lifestyle* has become a buzzword for the homosexual community, so I had no idea that in the days following my performance, participants in blogs and chat rooms began calling me antigay and homophobic.

That perception was sharpened when people discovered

that in a previous interview I had named Beth Moore as my American Idol. I mentioned Beth because she inspires me to live more like Jesus. But when people checked out her Web page, they discovered a link to Exodus International, an organization that supports people who want to leave the homosexual lifestyle.

My innocent use of the word *lifestyle*, combined with my admiration of Beth Moore and her support of a legitimate ministry, snowballed in the public's perception. At the time, I was blissfully unaware of the controversy, but it would soon rise up to haunt me.

Even knowing what I know now, I am glad I sang "Shackles." That song represents who I am, flaws and all, and I've never tried to be anything else up on a stage.

I was safe from elimination the week I sang "Shackles." I know now that many Christians were amazed at my boldness and responded by voting in droves. My girl Lisa Tucker was sent home, but the pain of parting was lessened by the assurance that we would see her again in a few months for the summer tour.

Simon called Lisa the "best sixteen-year-old" to ever audition for the show. I had always felt close to her and found it amusing that we got along so well—I, the oldest contestant, and she, the youngest.

Lisa is one of the most beautiful, intelligent, pure girls I know, and I hope to maintain a lasting relationship with her for many years. She handled her exit with style and grace.

I should have watched her more closely.

9 Losing Courage

After our week of songs from the twenty-first century, the *Idol* producers told us our next theme would be country music. But before we chose our country song, we had to prepare another number for the *following* week.

On the tail end of their six-week North American tour, Queen was scheduled to perform at the Anaheim Pond on April 3. Even though we would not be singing Queen's songs for two weeks, *Idol* producers jumped at the opportunity to film the Idols mixing it up with members of Queen.

We took a short trip from Hollywood to Anaheim to perform with members of the legendary band. I had chosen to sing "Who Wants to Live Forever?" because I fell in love with the words:

> *Who wants to live forever?*
> *Who wants to live forever?*

Who dares to love forever?
When love must die

But touch my tears with your lips
Touch my world with your fingertips
And we can have forever
And we can love forever
Forever is our today
Who waits forever anyway?

I'm not sure what the lead guitarist, Brian May, intended when he wrote this song, but I saw it as a beautiful expression of what waits for us once we finally leave this earth. Who wants to live forever? I do! I have often longed to leave this temporary world to finally live in the presence of my heavenly Father. I was sure the stirring I felt when I practiced the song with Debra Byrd would result in my most moving performance yet.

After I sang "Shackles," Paula said she would love to hear me sing with more vulnerability. Not only did "Who Wants to Live Forever?" offer a moving message, but it was also the perfect tune to feature the softer side of my voice.

As we pulled into the loading dock of Anaheim Pond, we remaining contestants realized that in less than four months we would be performing on the same stage Queen would dominate that night. I felt an adrenaline rush when we walked into the giant arena and I looked up at seventeen thousand empty seats. Colored lights flashed, and a haze of smoke drifted overhead as electric-guitar riffs and screaming vocals threatened to snap the sound barrier—or my eardrums.

On stage, Brian May, Roger Taylor, and Paul Rodgers (the lead singer of Bad Company, who had joined Queen on this tour), were jamming to "We Will Rock You." I have never been a huge fan of rock music, but seeing all that energy on stage made me appreciate the skill involved in what rock musicians do.

I'm not exactly sure what I was expecting, but ignorance had led me to believe that these rockers were going to be rude and conceited when they met us *Idol* hopefuls. Nothing could have been further from the truth. I was amazed and humbled by the outpouring of love and support those musicians demonstrated. They were some of the kindest, most patient, and helpful people I had met in a long time. They made each of us feel special and valuable. I looked forward to singing with them.

> I'm not exactly sure what I was expecting, but ignorance led me to believe that these rockers were going to be rude and conceited when they met us *Idol* hopefuls. Nothing could have been further from the truth.

After a few minutes of getting to know one another and discussing the plans for the day, we began to rehearse. The *Idol* cameramen set about capturing B-roll footage as we sang onstage with Queen. One by one we humbly joined the legendary group members and performed our songs. We couldn't help but feel a sense of energy as we stood on that enormous stage, surrounded by flashing lights and supported by strong drums, bass, and guitars. We "Idols" in the audience were treated to a bona fide rock concert with each performance. Queen week was going to be a blast.

After my eight friends finished their songs, it was finally my turn. I'd been chosen to go last because my song was different from the others. Instead of being accompanied by flashing lights and a full band, I would sing with Brian May at the piano and a single spotlight overhead. It would be an intimate and personal performance.

As I walked onto the stage, Brian greeted me with a warm hug. He told me he had heard a recording of my rehearsal and he'd been moved by my performance. I was humbled and honored by his gentleness and kindness. As crew members placed a single microphone stand near the front of the stage, Brian asked if I wouldn't mind moving the mic back so I could face him and we could communicate with each other.

I readily obliged. From the first minor chord to the final soaring notes, I sang and felt power surge through my trembling limbs. Brian and I were sharing an experience, and at the end of the song, I saw him wipe a tear from his eye.

"It's an honor for me to hear you sing my song," he said, and I quickly assured him that the honor was all mine.

"Your song," I told him, "moves me to my core."

As we left the arena, I knew that in two weeks I'd offer America the performance of my life. But first I had to get through country week.

I chose to sing Shania Twain's "Any Man of Mine" because it was an upbeat tune that lent itself to improvisation. I'll confess to feeling a certain amount of pressure during that week. After all, I was representing Nashville, the country-music capital of the world. I have never claimed to be a country singer—I'll save that title for Kellie and Bucky—but a girl can't help where she's from.

Not only was I feeling a little pressure to do Tennessee proud, but producers for *Access Hollywood* had contacted my friend Chandra and asked if they could come to a viewing party she was having that Tuesday. Hundreds of my friends from college, church, LifeWay, the Living Proof Live events, and

"Fiskites" I had never even met planned to gather in a conference room at Fisk to watch that night's episode. Chandra was delighted by their interest, so *Access Hollywood* sent a camera crew to tape the event and conduct interviews.

My need to be sharp had never been greater than it was on country music night. I strode onto the stage, then smiled and sang through "Any Man of Mine." I loved my song and had a good time during my performance, but apparently the judges didn't have a good time listening to it. Neither did the American audience.

For the first time, I went home that night feeling that I'd given a mediocre performance. I felt a real sense of shame, a feeling that I'd let down my family and all the friends gathered at Fisk.

Though I hadn't given a superlative performance, I hoped I'd done well enough to get by. If so, next week's Queen song would undoubtedly redeem me.

Looking for a little encouragement, I called my pastor, Dave Buehring, for our weekly check-in. We talked a few minutes about how things were going and how I was feeling about the competition.

Then he broke some distressing news. "I know you haven't been getting on the Internet since the show began—"

I caught my breath. "No, I haven't."

"Well, I wanted to make you aware of some of the things that have been going on."

From his tone, I knew he was about to give me bad news. He proceeded to tell me about the backlash from the homosexual community since my performance of "Shackles." As he spoke, I felt as if the walls of my room were closing in on me. Even as Dave prayed and asked the Lord to give me comfort and wisdom, I stared at the floor in shock and dismay.

Where had that accusation come from? Why had it come at all? God knew I didn't hate gay people, so why had He allowed this insane thing to happen?

At that moment I would have given anything to go on national television and tell the world that it was all a crazy mistake. I didn't hate gay people; I didn't hate *anybody*. When I said God was bigger than our problems, I had been talking about my *own* addiction.

How could anyone look at me—at my size—and not understand what I had meant?

But I had no time to deal with the situation. The competition continued, and we had to brace for another show. Someone else would soon be eliminated, and I had to prepare my heart to say good-bye to another of my friends.

No Time to Ponder

For the past three weeks the Lord had given me a name to pray for on the morning of the elimination show. Without fail, that person had been the one eliminated on live television that night.

On Wednesday morning, April 5, I woke early and prayed individually for every person remaining in the competition. I kept listening for the Lord to whisper a specific name, but since He remained silent, I prayed for everyone.

In hindsight, I can see how God used that early morning prayer experience to prepare me for my own departure, but I didn't have that assurance while I was praying. I remembered feeling that God had assured me I'd be in the top three, so I fully expected to be around for several more weeks.

Yet a strange premonition hovered over me that entire day. For no reason in particular I found myself telling people on the staff that I loved and appreciated them. As Nigel addressed us before the results show, I felt the urge to ask him if he *truly* cared for us. For some reason, I needed to hear that he did. He confirmed his love for us and put my mind at ease with his warm smile.

Now I can see that God was helping me say my good-byes before I knew I had a reason to.

After guest star Kenny Rodgers performed on the show that night, Ryan began the process of pulling out those who faced the prospect of elimination. On camera, he informed us that we would be put in groups of three. One group had the lowest number of votes, and the other two groups would be safe from elimination. One by one, he read the judges' comments from the previous night. By the time he had gone through all of us, we sat in three groups. Ace, Bucky, and Katharine huddled in the first group. Elliott, Paris, and I made up the second group. Group three was composed of Chris, Kellie, and Taylor.

When Ryan sent group three back to the couches, a sense of foreboding descended over me. Even though Ace, Bucky, and Kat had all been in the bottom three at some point and neither Elliott, Paris, nor I had, I knew something was up. The situation reminded me of what happened one night in *Idol*'s third season: Three of the so-called divas—Fantasia Barrino, Jennifer Hudson, and LaToya London—landed in the bottom three. The result shocked everyone.

When Ryan announced that Ace, Bucky, and Kat were safe, my stomach twisted into a knot that grew tighter when Ryan took us into a commercial break. Over the next three minutes, an uncomfortable silence spread throughout the room. I could see people talking, but I couldn't hear them through the cottony silence that had filled my head.

I barely noticed when Nigel walked up and wished us luck. I began to question everything. Had my performance been that bad? Had I misunderstood God's promise? I loved Paris's and Elliott's voices, and I knew both of them would have huge careers in the Soul/R&B market. I didn't want them to go, but I wasn't ready to go either. After all, God had told me I'd make it into the top three—right?

> Elliott and I held hands and stood at center stage. Then Ryan said the words I'd been dreading.

As we came back from the commercial break, Ryan sent Paris to the couches with the other safe contestants. Elliott and I held hands and stood at center stage. Then Ryan said the words I'd been dreading. I had been eliminated.

I felt as if every light in the auditorium had cut off except for the single spotlight boring a hole into my forehead. My legs began to quiver, as did my lip.

I looked at Ryan and saw sympathy in his eyes. It was official. I had to leave.

The cameras panned across Kat's and Chris's shocked faces. I heard a collective gasp from the crowd, followed by dense silence. My hand rose to cover my mouth and slowly the audience began to clap. Several people stood, and as I remained rooted to the floor, Ryan leaned in to point out that the crowd was giving me a standing ovation.

Somehow I found the courage to smile through my tears as the producers played clips from my journey through the *American Idol* experience. When the montage ended, Ryan gave me a crooked smile. "Now, Mandisa, will you sing us out?"

It's traditional for the eliminated contestant to end the show with their prepared song. I always thought it odd that contestants would be asked to sing the song that got them kicked to the curb!

Somehow I put a smile on my face and sang "Any Man of Mine" as my farewell. When I'd finished, the other contestants and the judges came over and nearly smothered me in embraces.

As Simon hugged me, he murmured a question in my ear: "Why on earth did you choose that song?"

As soon as the show ends, the eliminated contestant does an interview with Ty Treadway, a reporter from *American Idol Extra*. I was sweaty, teary, and still in shock, but I managed to pull my act together for a brief chat with Ty. When the interview finished, someone whisked me off to meet with a counselor— yes, really. He and I had talked before, so in my exit interview he said, "Of all the people here, you're the one I'm the least concerned about. You have a good foundation, and I know your faith is a big part of that."

I looked at him and decided to be bluntly honest. "That's right," I told him, "but right now I'm feelin' shaky because I feel like the Lord told me something that didn't happen. I don't know if He changed His mind or if I heard Him wrong."

Sitting there, I questioned everything from God's sovereignty to why I was eliminated. I had felt so *certain* I would make it to the top three. What had gone wrong? Should I blame it on my choice of a gospel song the previous week? Maybe it had something to do with the homosexual controversy raging on so many blogs. Had my country song really been so awful, or should I blame my elimination on my weight?

I didn't have much time to reason things out because staffers kept me hustling from one interview to another. The exit procedure is nearly as grueling as the competition. I left the

counselor and immediately faced additional interviews with
TV Guide Channel and other shows. Those were really difficult
because my mom, dad, stepmom,
aunt, and cousin stood in the background and looked on while I talked.
I kept a smile on my face and pretended to be okay, but I wasn't okay
at all. I wanted to crawl in a hole and
stay there.

> I kept a smile
> on my face and
> pretended to be
> okay, but I wasn't
> okay at all.

An Italian Send-Off

The situation went from bad to worse. The live show had taped
at 5:30 p.m. on the West Coast, and after the interviews, I still
had to attend what we laughingly called the "kiss-off dinner,"
held in a private room of a local Italian restaurant.

I didn't arrive until sometime between nine and ten o'clock.
I looked around and saw scattered tables filled with my fellow
contestants, their guests, and *Idol* staff. The room buzzed with
conversation and laughter while the scents of Italian spices
wafted on the air.

My dad and stepmom had left earlier to catch their flight
home, so my mom, aunt, and cousin joined me at a table. I
knew what would come next. As in previous kiss-off dinners,
we would feast on pasta, chicken parmesan, and garlic bread,
then each of the contestants and staff would take turns toast-
ing (and sometimes roasting) the eliminated contestant.

Now it was my turn, and despite my smile, I didn't feel
ready.

Taylor stood and grinned at me. "Now that you're gone,
Mandisa, we're all going to hell." He was joking, so after everyone laughed, he went on to say that I was the one keeping

everybody in line. In a more serious tone, he said it meant a lot to know I was praying for them.

Ace said I was the cleanest person he'd ever met (I think he meant *pure*). Paris likened me to a big sister. Kellie dissolved into a puddle of tears but composed herself enough to say I was one of the godliest women she had ever known and she looked up to me very much.

The things they said were so affirming; they let me know I had been more than a fellow contestant. They saw me as someone who was walking out her Christian faith.

And that, I realized, was exactly what I had asked the Lord to let me be.

After each person spoke, my spirits began to rise. When I finally stood to address the people I had come to love, I was so full of emotion I could barely speak. I told them how much their words meant to me. I said the Lord had awakened me that morning so I could pray for each of them, and I'd made a vow to continue to pray for them for the rest of my life. I said it had been an honor to have been part of what I considered to be the best season of *American Idol*. As an *Idol* fanatic, I knew I could say that without bias.

In closing, I told them that I expected great things from each of them and I wouldn't say good-bye because I knew we'd be touring together in a few months. I looked around the room, imprinting each of their dear faces into my memory. "So I'll see you all soon."

> It had been an honor to have been part of what I considered to be the best season of *American Idol*.

As irreverent as it sounds, the "kiss-off dinner" is a great thing. Most people don't receive those kinds of affirmations until after they're dead, and by then it's too late. My mom wept as my friends spoke, and I really enjoyed the tender experience. It was a good night after all.

After the dinner, a staffer whisked me back to the apartment to pack my belongings. I had a 4 a.m. call time to begin my press week, so I stayed up all night. Kellie was a mess. She lay across my bed and cried, but I told her to go to sleep; she'd need her strength for the next day.

It had been a difficult night—an emotional roller coaster—but I was too numb to think much about it.

Too Numb to Pray

I had asked God to use my offering of the song "Shackles," but I wanted him to use it according to the scenario I had dreamed up. I had no idea He would use it to ignite a firestorm that threatened to burn me alive.

The next morning I was escorted to a room where for nearly three hours I did a series of radio interviews.

I hadn't slept, and I still hadn't dealt with my disappointment over my elimination. All the time I was packing, I kept trying to talk to the Lord, but the only words that came out were, "I don't understand what happened. What went wrong?"

I had not had a chance to be quiet and still and let the Lord speak to me.

After the radio interviews, an escort took me to another location where I did interviews with *Extra, Access Hollywood,* and other shows I can't even remember. Then the car dropped me off at a hotel for a couple of hours to freshen up for my appearance on the *Tonight Show with Jay Leno.*

Someone from the *Tonight Show* staff showed me and my assigned publicist to the green room, where we would wait for the interview. My publicist sat in a chair against the wall while I sank into a beige sofa. I felt as if my entire body had been given a dose of Novocain. Though I was looking forward to whatever antics Jay had up his sleeve, I was utterly exhausted.

I had just closed my eyes to catch a moment of rest when another publicist came in and informed me that he was calling *The Advocate* for a short telephone interview while I waited for my segment.

I was surprised that a gay periodical would be interested in interviewing me, but I was in no position to question the assignment. A moment later I straightened my spine and accepted the phone, greeting my interviewer with a cheerful, "Hi, there!"

After a few routine questions about my song selection, which of the other contestants I would miss, and what my future plans included, the interviewer got down to the real reason for his call. He asked about my appreciation for the "antigay writer and lecturer Beth Moore."

I drew a deep breath and told him Beth had been a huge influence in my life and I respected her as a teacher and a woman of God.

"Would you be comfortable performing or singing at a gay event?" the reporter asked.

I said I would not feel comfortable in that situation.

"Would it conflict with your religious beliefs?"

I said I wasn't an advocate for homosexuality.

The reporter kept pounding me with questions, and his tone, which had been pleasant, became decidedly sharp. "Before you sang the Mary Mary gospel song 'Shackles,' you mentioned that people's various addictions and lifestyles are not as strong as God. Were you speaking of gay people?"

I explained that I'd been heartbroken when I heard how my

comments had been misinterpreted. I said that I try to treat others the way I'd want be treated. I hate no one.

I'd been heartbroken when I heard how my comments had been misinterpreted.

"That song is a very personal testimony for me," I continued. "I've been dealing with an addiction to food for most of my life. I've been living a lifestyle of pure indulgence, giving in to every desire I've had as far as what I've put into my body. I don't need a diet; what I need is a lifestyle change. So when I said that, I was speaking of how the Lord is helping me overcome my personal struggles. I was saying that if God can do that for me—and a lot of other people face different things—He can do it for anybody."

With that we ended the interview, but the topic came up again and again as I continued on the publicity junket.

When I was finally alone in my hotel room, I called room service and ordered a hamburger, french fries, and cheesecake. Overwhelmed with confusion, I stuffed myself while I tried to be honest with the Lord.

Maybe I binged because I was angry. I knew God could handle my anger, so I poured out my feelings and let Him know exactly what I was thinking and feeling.

When I had finished eating everything on my plate, I lay on the floor and wailed aloud before the Lord. "You lied to me," I cried, and then I realized God doesn't lie. Since God *can't* lie, the fault had to lie in me. I must not have heard His voice correctly—and what kind of Christian could I be if I couldn't hear the Lord?

At that point I wasn't even hearing from my friends. Though they called, I isolated myself from the people who loved me. I didn't answer phone calls, because I didn't want to deal with sympathy and I didn't want to hear pep talks. So I remained alone, bewildered, stressed, and depressed.

The next day I flew to New York to be on *Live with Regis and Kelly*, *Fox and Friends*, CNN, and other network programs.

That's where I did a radio interview in which a woman yelled at me for being a "gay basher." She said, "You say you try to live a life guided by love, but how is it loving to say someone needs to be changed?"

> I isolated myself from the people who loved me. I didn't answer phone calls because I didn't want to deal with sympathy and I didn't want to hear pep talks.

"I believe you can love someone and not agree with everything they do," I answered.

I couldn't understand why she was so angry and vehement. People kept accusing me of hating, yet they seemed to hate me with a passion.

The firestorm only worsened my feelings of disappointment about being eliminated. There were moments in that week when I thought everyone in America had turned against me. One DJ on Fox radio—a self-proclaimed "Jesus-loving freak"— applauded me for my stand, but he was the exception.

Every interviewer I met that week asked about the gay controversy. I explained that I have never wanted to be characterized by hate; I want to love everyone into the Kingdom. I've seen those people who carry signs saying "God Hates Fags," and that attitude breaks my heart. God loves everyone, and as a follower of Jesus, I am determined to love people too.

Over and over, I tried to make my position clear. "As a born-again Christian, I believe the Bible is the accurate Word of God, and I try to live my life according to the principles outlined

in it," I told interviewer after interviewer. "Sometimes I suc-
ceed. Sometimes I fail. But being perfect is not what makes me
a Christian. Being in a relationship with the one holy God is
what makes me a Christian. I believe anyone who asks Jesus to
save them and be the Lord of his or her life is saved. Sin is sin,
and all of it displeases God. One day we are all going to face a
judge, but His name will not be Mandisa."

I traveled through that week in a daze, stating my position countless times, trying to explain that I hadn't meant to
hurt anyone. My words fell mainly on deaf ears because most
people had already made up their minds about who I was and
what I represented.

The experience was alternately heartbreaking and frustrating, but I shouldn't have been surprised. Jesus went about the
country doing good, and He was misunderstood too. He spoke
of loving one's neighbor and loving God, yet people were constantly trying to trap Him and twist His words.

My mind went back to one of the psalms, and I wondered if
Jesus thought of it when He was misunderstood:

> *They are always twisting what I say;*
> *they spend their days plotting to harm me.*
>
> PSALM 56:5

And then I remembered the lovely promise found only a few
verses later:

> *You keep track of all my sorrows.*
> *You have collected all my tears in your bottle.*
> *You have recorded each one in your book.*
>
> PSALM 56:8

I have never suffered to the extent Jesus did, but after that week of exit interviews, I began to understand how His heart ached when people looked at Him with hate and anger in their eyes.

Retreating from the World

After a hectic week of exit interviews and only a few hours of sleep, I flew home to Nashville. Several people on the plane recognized me and said things like, "We couldn't believe you got voted off" or "You were robbed."

I have never suffered to the extent Jesus did, but after that week of exit interviews, I began to understand how His heart ached when people looked at Him with hate and anger in their eyes.

I've heard a lot of those comments over the last year, and trust me, I'd much rather hear that than "Girlfriend, it was past time for you to go."

My friends called to ask how I wanted to arrive back home. Did I want a party, or did I want to sneak back into town? Since I was in a really bad place, I wanted to see a few close friends and no one else. So when I walked off the plane, I stepped into the arms of Travis and Angela Cottrell with their kids Jack, Lily Kate, and Levi; Chance and Jennifer Scoggins; and my pastor, Dave Buehring, and his wife, Cheryl. They were all waiting on the other side of the security checkpoint.

When they hugged me, I was reminded what unconditional love felt like. We went to my favorite restaurant, the Cheesecake Factory, and I stuffed myself again. My friends wanted to talk honestly and openly, but I wasn't ready to broach the subject of my elimination. They encouraged me to open up, but I wasn't at the point where I could share my feelings. They understood and assured me they would be around when I was ready.

Finally, I went home and sat in the silence of my apartment. As thoughts of the Lord crept into my head, I pushed them down and ignored them, turning instead to the TV and mindless programming. My luggage sat by the front door, right where I'd dropped it, because I didn't have the heart to unpack. I couldn't find the strength or the heart to do anything.

That night, as I lay in bed and drifted at the edge of sleep, the Lord tried again to get my attention. But I shut Him out by turning my thoughts to what I had done wrong in the competition. Maybe I shouldn't have sung "Shackles." Or maybe I was supposed to sing the song but wasn't supposed to make comments as I walked onstage.

Maybe I should have kept my mouth shut and not said anything to anyone. I wouldn't have been much of a testimony, but I wouldn't have offended anyone either.

Why had God brought me down this road only to have the dream end so abruptly? Why had He allowed this crazy homosexuality issue to swirl around me? I didn't know anything about homosexuality, and I certainly never meant to be perceived as a woman on a crusade against gay people.

My emotions veered from confusion to anger. "Why, Father?" I shouted the words in the quiet of the apartment. "Why did You do this to me? It would have been nice if You'd led me into some issue where I felt better prepared. Why couldn't You have sent interviewers from the National Association to Advance Fat Acceptance instead of *The Advocate*? Why couldn't You place me in circles where I feel *comfortable?*"

But maybe . . . He'd put me where I'd have to depend on Him.

I turned and snuggled in my pillow, not wanting to hear from God. I thought I *had been* depending on the Lord. I had begged Him to open up the windows of heaven and pour out blessings on everyone who roomed with me or heard me sing from the time I reached Hollywood until the time I hit the top three—or had that been *my* plan?

No answers came. I languished in my pitiful weakness and didn't leave the apartment for several days. I sheltered myself for a long time—ordered a lot of pizza, slept too much, and didn't bathe. Didn't unpack, either; I only slept, ate, and watched TV.

When the phone rang, I ignored it and let the answering machine take a message. Soon I began to hear people saying, "We just want to know if you're alive."

My best friend, Chandra, would call to say she was on her way over to check on me. I'd call Chandra back and tell her to turn around because I didn't want to talk and wouldn't answer the door.

The Dark Night of the Soul

I know that some of you have probably lowered your estimation of my spiritual maturity over the last couple of pages. You may find it hard to believe that a grown woman could collapse like a house of cards just because she got voted off some TV contest.

Others of you may be thinking it was a good thing I didn't have a husband and kids, or I wouldn't have the luxury of being able to *hold* a solitary pity party. If you have kept a vigil by the bedside of a dying child or spouse, you might think my behavior childish, spoiled, or illogical.

What can I say? If I'd been another person or in another place, I might not have reacted as I did. I might not have auditioned for *American Idol* at all. But I am who I am, and sometimes we experience emotions that defy logical explanation.

St. John of the Cross, a Spanish mystic and poet who lived

in the sixteenth century, wrote a theological treatise called *The Dark Night of the Soul.* I haven't read the work, but I've seen it referred to a number of times. The title is enough to make people nod knowingly if they've experienced one of those dark nights.

I find it comforting to realize that I'm not the only one who has experienced a time of depression and spiritual dryness.

"When I was in seminary," writes Stephen Eyre, in *Drawing Close to God,* "I went through a period of four years during which God seemed absent. I believe that God wanted my theological learning to be more than an academic experience. In the midst of this time I began to understand why St. John of the Cross called it 'the dark night of the soul.'"[1]

"We all experience periods of spiritual coldness," agrees R. C. Sproul, "in which we feel as if God has totally removed the light of his countenance from us. The saints have called it the 'dark night of the soul.' There are times when we feel as if God has abandoned us. We think that he no longer hears our prayers. We do not feel the sweetness of his presence."[2]

Moses, who talked with God and saw dozens of amazing miracles, was once so frustrated and in despair that he cried to the Almighty, "If this is how you intend to treat me, just go ahead and kill me. Do me a favor and spare me this misery!" (Numbers 11:15).

I understand how each of these men felt. My chief complaint against the Lord was that I felt he'd misled me. After several days at home I wasn't even talking to Him. I felt that He'd abandoned me. I doubted His intentions toward me.

When He tried to get my attention in the silence of the night, I turned up the volume on my sleep machine to drown Him out. I was angry with Him. Another part of me felt ashamed because I'd obviously gotten something wrong.

I kept remembering why I hadn't told anyone about my involvement in the Star 94 contest—I kept that situation secret because I didn't want to disappoint anyone. Because I *couldn't* keep *Idol* a secret, I had disappointed everyone.

I felt a lot like Cain, condemned to wandering from place to place as punishment for killing his brother. I hadn't committed murder, but I related to Cain's guilt and loneliness (see Genesis 4:10-15). If I could have flown to a place where not even God can go, I'd have been first in line to buy a ticket.

Despite my anger and depression, though, I couldn't forget the words of David. I had memorized one of his psalms years ago, so even though I hadn't opened my Bible in weeks, the words haunted me as I slept:

I kept remembering why I hadn't told anyone about my involvement in the Star 94 contest— I kept that situation secret because I didn't want to disappoint anyone. Because I *couldn't* keep *Idol* secret, I had disappointed everyone.

> *O LORD, you have examined my heart and know*
> *everything about me.*
> *You know when I sit down or stand up. You know my*
> *every thought when far away.*
> *You chart the path ahead of me and tell me where to*
> *stop and rest. Every moment you know where I am.*
> *You know what I am going to say even before I say it,*
> *LORD.*
> *You both precede and follow me. You place your hand*
> *of blessing on my head.*

*Such knowledge is too wonderful for me, too great for
    me to know!*
*I can never escape from your spirit! I can never get
    away from your presence!*
*If I go up to heaven, you are there; if I go down to the
    place of the dead, you are there.*
*If I ride the wings of the morning, if I dwell by the far-
    thest oceans, even there your hand will guide me,
    and your strength will support me.*
*I could ask the darkness to hide me and the light
    around me to become night—but even in darkness I
    cannot hide from you.*
*To you the night shines as bright as day. Darkness and
    light are both alike to you.*

PSALM 139:1-12

I didn't read much Scripture during those dark days after my
return from California, but that psalm is imprinted on the lin-
ing of my heart. Those words hemmed in my anger and confusion; they kept me safe. I allowed myself to be angry with God
because I knew the Lord wasn't afraid of my anger. I allowed
myself to question Him because I knew He was bigger than my
questions. As hard as His answers might be to accept, I knew
they had my best interest at heart and one day I would understand. But in April 2006, that day seemed very far away.

10 In the Lord's Thoughts

Now when I look back, I wince at how quickly, suddenly, and completely I folded when I hit a bump in the road. God was still working in His way and in His time, but I was too busy grieving to see it.

I know God is sovereign. I know the Lord "causes everything to work together for the good of those who love God and are called according to His purpose for them" (Romans 8:28). I know that God's children often find themselves in a storm. Sometimes God calms the storm (see Mark 4:39). Sometimes He allows us to triumph over the storm by calling us to walk on water (see Matthew 14:29). Sometimes He gives us the strength to weather the storm (see Acts 27:27-41).

In the spring and summer following my elimination from *American Idol*, however, I didn't want to think about God's reasons for allowing me to go through a storm. My circumstances looked a lot different from what I thought they would, and I didn't understand why God would put me in the middle of a downpour.

I didn't want to think about anything, but being human, I couldn't shut off my brain. No matter how I tried to bury myself in mindless television, binging, or sleep, my thoughts kept returning to my time at *American Idol*. The competition replayed in my dreams, so I'd wake in the gray light of morning and feel like I'd just left a room filled with contestants.

It was painful for me to watch the remaining weeks of the show, but like an asthmatic smoker who can't let go of her cigarettes, I couldn't resist.

The first week was the most difficult to endure. I sat in my living room and hugged a pillow as the remaining eight contestants performed their Queen songs. Tears filled my eyes as I recalled each precious moment of our rehearsal. I had been there, but every sign of me had been carefully edited out of the B-roll footage they showed before each performance.

The most gut-wrenching part of the hour was watching Kat sing "Who Wants to Live Forever?" She had every right to sing that song, and she gave a beautiful and moving performance. Still, I cried. I couldn't help feeling wounded and jealous because I'd chosen that song first. Why wasn't *I* singing that song?

A couple of days later, Chance left me a message saying that he heard Brian May was trying to get in touch with me. With my curiosity piqued, I searched the Internet for Brian's Web site and was shocked to learn that he maintains an online blog.

When I read his entry for April 10, my heart lightened for a brief moment: "I am only sad . . . that you won't be seeing

Mandisa with us guys. . . . If you're out there, Mandisa, send me a message, okay? We all feel for you so much. . . . You getting ruled out of the game was honestly the last thing I expected."

I e-mailed him to thank him for his shout-out, and he responded with more encouragement than my heart could handle. For the first time since being eliminated, I felt affirmed and valuable.

Over the following weeks, I watched as Bucky, Ace, Kellie, Paris, Chris, and Elliott were sent home. Like most people, I was stunned the night Chris was eliminated. But in my horrible state of mind, I selfishly wished it hadn't happened because now *his* elimination, not mine, would be remembered as the shocker of season five.

Great. Another weight to add to the emotions keeping me bogged down in the pit of guilt and despair.

After returning home, I remained in a funk until I *had* to pick myself up and come back for the *Idol* finale in May. Even then I still hadn't accepted the work of God's hand in my life, and it wasn't until I finished the top-ten tour in September that I really came to terms with what had happened to me.

The Pit and the Pizza Boxes

One afternoon, as I sat at my computer playing a challenging game of Spider Solitaire, a familiar *ding* startled me: I had a new e-mail.

Grateful for a reason to close the losing game, I clicked on my in-box and found a message from a woman whose name I did not recognize. She opened by saying, "Mandisa, you do not know me."

Since being eliminated from *American Idol,* I had received floods of e-mails from well-wishers attempting to console me.

Some of their messages I read; many I deleted. I answered none of them.

But this particular woman continued by saying that she'd received my e-mail address from a friend who used to work with me at LifeWay. She proceeded to tell me that I had inspired her because she, too, was a heavy woman, and she considered me to be the most beautiful person she'd ever seen.

I groaned and looked in the mirror. It had been a long time since I'd put on makeup. My braids were tangled and unkempt, my face was swollen because I'd been sleeping too much, and my purple sweats were wrinkled and smelly because I'd not bathed in days.

I reread the line about how beautiful I was. Then I deleted the message, turned off my computer, and walked to the phone to order a pizza.

As I walked, the familiar words to "Shackles" filled my mind:

> *Everything that could go wrong*
> *All went wrong at one time*
> *So much pressure fell on me*
> *I thought I was gon' lose my mind*
> *But I know You wanna see*
> *If I will hold on through these trials*
> *But I need You to lift this load*
> *'Cause I can't take it no more.*

I hung my head and wept. I'd sung that song so many times that the words were as much a part of me as my skin, but I wasn't living what I'd sung. Everything had gone wrong, and instead of holding on through the trials, I had let go.

I'd tumbled into the pit of despair, reaching for pizza boxes and bags of munchies instead of the Word of God. Instead of calling on the Lord to lift me out, I kept dialing Papa John's in an effort to fill my needs.

I leaned against the kitchen counter as I dropped into the well of memory. Just after Tameka had been eliminated, I had sat on the edge of her bed and told myself that she was a mature believer so she would have no problem handling her disappointment.

> Instead of calling on the Lord to lift me out, I kept dialing Papa John's in an effort to fill my needs.

I was a mature believer, too, so why was I having problems?

I lifted my head and shouted at the Lord. "It's because You told me I'd make the top three! If You hadn't told me that, I'd be fine!"

Nothing rumbled from heaven in rebuke or answer, so I sank into a chair and remembered another time I'd sat alone like this. That day I'd had a praise party instead of worrying about whether or not I'd made it into the top forty-four. In my journal I'd written that I'd learned a lesson for life—win or lose, I could feel peace if I worshipped the Lord in the midst of sorrow and despair.

But I had never felt less like worshipping.

Thoughts of my journal reminded me of what I'd read in my devotional book: *Should we accept only good things from the hand of God and never anything bad?*

Whether I turned to the right or to the left, my own memories, thoughts, and songs convicted me of my failure. But I had fallen into a deep pit, and I couldn't see any light overhead.

Even so, the Lord had not forgotten me.

Over the next several days I continued questioning myself and the Lord. Then the words of a beloved and familiar passage of Scripture came to me: "When I was a child, I spoke and thought and reasoned as a child. But when I grew up, I put away childish things. Now we see things imperfectly as in a cloudy mirror, but then we will see everything with perfect clarity. All that I know now is partial and incomplete, but then I will know everything completely, just as God now knows me completely" (1 Corinthians 13:11-12).

The more I thought about it, the more I realized that if I heard God perfectly every time He spoke, I'd either be a perfect person or in a perfect place. And since neither situation is true, the blame for the miscommunication between me and God had to lie in my ears—and my heart.

I stood on the imperfect side of eternity, with mortal ears and strong desires. Sometimes God spoke and I heard him; at other times I heard what I wanted to hear. Maybe I filled in the blanks of God's silence with what I wanted Him to say because although I really didn't want to become the American Idol, I *did* want to make it into the top three. That would have been my childhood dream come true.

The little girl who told disbelieving friends she wanted to be a singer would have been able to say, "Look! I made it. I told you I would!"

But God didn't want me to accomplish my dreams in my own strength. He wanted me to end up exactly where I did . . . so He could prove Himself.

Through a Glass Darkly

We are imperfect people living in an imperfect world. One day I will understand with complete clarity, but until then, I have to trust the God who leads me through the sunlight and the shadow.

Listening for and responding to God's voice is what life's faith journey is all about. But I've asked the Lord for a favor once I get to heaven.

Many people will want to walk hand in hand with the Lord in a beautiful garden laden with greenery and filled with unusual creatures. Others will want to dine at a table loaded with a glorious feast and converse with Him over dinner. (And I will be tempted to join them if there's cheesecake for dessert!) But I'd like Jesus to set up a movie screen in a private theater where He and I can watch a replay of my life and several other historical moments.

I've seen all of the movies about the life of Moses, but I want to see the Red Sea part before my eyes.[1] I would like to see the expression on Balaam's face when the donkey turned to rebuke him.[2] I'd like to observe the afternoon when Paul preached so long the young man perched on the upstairs window ledge fell asleep and hit the ground outside—and was brought back to life by the power of God.[3]

As for my own life, I want to revisit those places where I have mentally set up a marker. When the Lord and I sit down to review my DVR (Divine Video Replay), I want to revisit those points and ask the Lord for permission to know what was going on in the spiritual realm as I passed through that milestone of my life's journey.

I want to see the near accidents He helped me avoid. I want to witness my heavenly Father's anger and heartbreak as my friend's neighbor stole my virginity. I want to see and hear the angelic celebration that took place after the "Singing Christmas Tree" when I walked down the aisle to give my life to Jesus.

I want to know how Satan felt when I sang "Shackles" and testified of God's power to thirty million viewers. I want to know if any people had their faith enlarged by my simple words of introduction.

I hope there were many—and trust that's why Satan instigated that sneak attack, intending to distract me with having to find another performance outfit moments before I went on the air. I believe he trembled at the potential for good, and that's why he later reveled in my depression over hostile reporters who hounded me about being antigay.

> As days and weeks passed, I began to see that my elimination wasn't God's punishment for my presumption or some other sin. My ninth-place finish is what God intended all along.

Scripture tells us that God shows "his wisdom in its rich variety to all the unseen rulers and authorities in the heavenly places" (Ephesians 3:10). In eternity, I'm looking forward to hearing the Lord's explanation and seeing the full revelation of life's mysteries.

As days and weeks passed, I began to see that my elimination wasn't God's punishment for my presumption or for some other sin. My ninth-place finish is what God intended all along: "The LORD directs the steps of the godly. He delights in every detail of their lives. Though they stumble, they will never fall, for the LORD holds them by the hand" (Psalm 37:23-24).

> I'm *not* an American pop star. I'm a plus-sized, thirty-year-old black woman whose heart belongs to Jesus.

I am *not* an American pop star. I'm a plus-sized, thirty-year-old black woman whose heart belongs to Jesus. My ultimate goal in life involves more than music—I would welcome the opportunity to be a speaker or Bible teacher. I'd love to be able to take the life lessons I've learned and teach them to younger women.

The world has enough singers. What the world lacks are people who are willing to be transparent in their walk with Jesus. I want everything from my music to this book to point to the Lord and reveal how I've come to understand that, even in difficult times, Jesus is there and He has a purpose for everything.

I feel as if I accomplished my primary goal for my *Idol* experience— to "walk my talk" and minister in some way to the other contestants and people I met as a result of being on the show.

I've heard many theories about why I was eliminated in ninth place. Some say the homosexual lobby turned against me; others feel it was because my weight didn't fit the "*Idol* image." Some blame my lackluster performance during country-music week. Some people maintain that my outspoken support of the gospel earned me a ticket home. Others claim I was voted out because some of my fans thought I was a shoo-in and voted for other contestants that week.

I've heard everything from racism to technical malfunction given as a reason for my elimination, but you know what? I went home in the ninth round because that's how God chose to work out His plan for my life. I don't know how He worked out the details, but I rest in the knowledge that all things work for the good of those who love God.

Of course, it's one thing to say those words—and another to live them.

Ministering on the Top Ten Tour

In June 2006, the top-ten Idols reunited for our three-month tour. I was still struggling with depression, but I pulled my act together and went on tour, glad for a chance to reconnect with my friends. Before I left Nashville, my pastor gave me a discipleship workbook he had written.

So I wrote invitations to all the contestants, suggesting that we do a Bible study every Sunday during the time we'd be riding from the hotel to the arena. If anyone was interested, I said, they should let me know.

The girls were interested. So one Sunday, as we pulled out from the hotel and looked forward to our concert, the other girls and I gathered in the bus to study God's Word. We turned the back of that tour bus into a sanctuary as we closed the door that led to the bunks. The small lounge area smelled of diesel fuel, so one of the girls lit an apple-cinnamon candle.

We women, plus Lisa's brother, Billy, and Paris's mom, Jamecia, lounged on the green patent-leather couches as I opened my Bible. Kellie crunched quietly on Honey Bunches of Oats cereal as I opened the meeting in prayer.

Our first devotional focused on the topic of relationships—girls are never reluctant to talk about relationships. We began by naming the things people need for a healthy relationship. We jotted down an exhaustive list and agreed that three of the most important things in a healthy relationship are communication, quality time, and honesty.

"A relationship with Jesus requires the same things," I told them. "We communicate with Him through prayer, and prayer isn't just dropping to your knees to offer up a wish list. Prayer happens all through the day. If you're frustrated about something, tell Jesus. If you're grateful, thank Him."

Our first meeting went well because all the girls were open and receptive. I was brutally honest and told them I was still having a hard time with everything that had happened after my elimination.

"Though I know God is in control," I said, "I know it with my *head*, not my heart. But I know if I reestablish my daily communication, quality time, and honesty with the Lord, my emotions will come around to where they should be."

That devotional series renewed my relationship with Jesus. Though the idea had come from my pastor, I knew I wanted to be more than just another singer on the bus. I wanted to minister, and though I told the Lord I still wasn't "feeling it," I would obey and lead those devotional hours. That's when I learned that even when you don't feel like doing something, God will honor your obedience.

We continued our devotional study the next week with a talk about trust in relationships. One of the girls opened up to me privately and shared that she was having a hard time with trust. That study had been meant for her.

The Lord used the most mundane things to illustrate His points. On that particular Sunday, Lisa was understandably upset because her luggage had disappeared. She was worried and afraid that someone had stolen hers and Billy's things. On the bus, we prayed and asked the Lord to find Lisa's luggage.

After we arrived at the arena, I was walking to the dressing room when Lisa came running up to tell me someone had found her bags. I gave her a smile as big as Texas, grateful for this small proof that the Lord had heard and responded to my prayer. That was a simple thing, but it was a turning point for me. Just what I needed to bolster my weary faith.

Can faith grow weary? Sure it can. The Bible is filled with stories of people who prayed and waited years for those prayers to be answered. Sarah waited long past the age of childbearing before she gave birth to her promised son, Isaac. The children of Israel spent generations in bondage in Egypt. The Hebrews of Daniel's generation suffered through exile in Babylon for seventy years before the Lord allowed them to return to their Promised Land.

In each case, God had His reasons for waiting before He answered the prayers of His people. I'm sure many faith-filled people have begged heaven for an answer to their prayers— and grown weary as they waited on God.

But God is faithful, and He does not measure time as we do. Furthermore, He sees the beginning, the middle, and the end of our lives, and He knows what is best for us better than we ever could.

Our sixty-city *American Idol* tour ended on September 24, 2006, a full year after I auditioned in Chicago. As I look back on those months, I can see how 2006 proved to be a pivotal year for me. My life changed because God led me to *American Idol,* and I know it will continue to change in new and unexpected ways. Those changes won't happen because of *Idol.* They'll come because I'm walking with the Lord and experiencing every day as an adventure.

Heard It through the Grapevine

Since returning home from the American Idols Live tour, one aspect of my new life adventure is learning how to live with celebrity. In addition to the occasional invasion of my physical privacy, it has also struck me as odd that people think they can say anything about you if you're famous and somehow it won't hurt. Or they can make a rude remark when you're standing two feet away and not expect you to hear.

Kellie and I had several conversations about this during the show. A couple of nights she came to my room, upset about something someone said about her in a magazine or on TV. Comments about her being "stupid" or "fake" hurt her feelings, and reporters' delving into her family history felt like an invasion of privacy.

Every now and then I will stumble across an article about me on the Web. I usually try to click it off immediately because I don't like how most articles make me feel.

I read a short biography about me on a Web site, and it reported that in the summer of 2007 I would be starring in a movie with Lindsay Lohan. That was news to me! Another site incorrectly listed my middle name and birthday. Those things are no big deal, but every now and then I read something that rocks my world, and that's no fun.

I'll never forget reading one particular article shortly after I was eliminated. The writer asserted that the reason I was sent home had nothing to do with my voice or song choice. It was because America hates fat people. After he went into graphic detail about my disgusting weight problem, I decided that I would never read anything else having to do with me, good or bad. If I read negative articles, I tend to get depressed, and positive articles tend to puff up my ego. I don't want anyone but the Lord to dictate my worth, and I sure don't want to walk around with a swelled head!

Before *Idol*, I used to rattle on about contestants on reality shows, but now I've realized how crazy it is to form opinions about people without really knowing them. I used to buy those magazines that brag about their exclusive pictures of celebrities shopping, on vacation, or stepping out of their front doors without makeup.

Then one day I had a paparazzo follow me into an Ashley

Stewart store as I shopped for a new performance outfit. I couldn't believe that the amount I paid for a black dress would be considered newsworthy, let alone that the video would later be plastered on a gossip Web site.

It's almost as if our society believes that celebrities aren't normal people or that they're breathing mannequins who are impervious to our words and actions.

I've learned that achieving a small measure of fame doesn't change who you really are. It can, however, help you develop a thick skin, and it can help you realize who your true friends are: They're the ones who loved you before you were on television.

> I've learned that achieving a small measure of fame doesn't change who you really are. It can, however, help you develop a thick skin, and it can help you realize who your true friends are—they're the ones who loved you before you were on television.

Fame has also reminded me of the importance of living a life that pleases God above all else. Paul wrote the Philippians this encouragement: "Do everything without complaining and arguing, so that no one can criticize you. Live clean, innocent lives as children of God, shining like bright lights in a world full of crooked and perverse people." (Philippians 2:14-15).

Sometimes I can't believe that thousands of people know who I am—and that I have an entry in Wikipedia. Fame has allowed me to explore new opportunities, but I've lost the freedom to step out of my house without makeup or in my sweats.

Celebrity and the Peril of Plenty

Everything is a trade-off, and I've had to be careful that I don't exchange the trivial for treasures.

When I worked in customer service at LifeWay, my ministry extended about as far as my telephone line. Until I began to sing at Living Proof Live events and at the occasional church, the only people I really ministered to were my callers.

But I *loved* talking to the people who called our customer-support line. On a nearly daily basis I was given the opportunity to lift some-one's needs to the Father.

Fame has allowed me to explore new opportunities, but I've lost the freedom to step out of my house without makeup or in my sweats.

One day a woman called to order ten *Breaking Free* workbooks by Beth Moore. Since that was the first of Beth's studies that I'd done, I asked the lady if she was do-ing the study for the first time. She emphatically informed me that she'd already gone through the workbook with some of her friends and would soon be leading a group of recovering alco-holics through the same life-changing study.

I told her that my life had changed after completing that study too. I said that I'd realized Jesus came to set the captives free and that He truly cared about His children in bondage. I encouraged her in her mission and prayed with her for the ten ladies who would be joining her in the study.

Over that phone line we laughed. We cried. We bonded. By the time I said good-bye, the call timer showed that I had spo-ken to her for almost an hour! (I suppose that's why they even-tually moved me from the order line to a sales position.)

But handling calls like that one reminded me that I was a vessel in the Lord's service. The devotional time I enjoyed every morning was a filling experience that allowed me to overflow onto the people I met, even if I met them on the phone.

But financially? I was barely scraping by in those days. I

used to groan every time I spied my bank's return address on a piece of mail, because I was forever emptying my bank account and bouncing checks. I tried hard to follow my mom's example and use cents-off coupons to save money on groceries, but I was too lazy to make a real effort at it. My father had given me a car when I went away to college, but because I didn't maintain it properly, the poor thing was in major need of intensive—and expensive—care.

Yet despite my financial insecurity, I have never experienced more joy and peace than I did in those lean years. I woke at five every morning to ensure I'd have ample time to study my Bible and pray before work. God and I met every morning, and my fellowship with Him didn't end when I began my workday. I would consistently talk with Him, often whispering, "Thank you, Lord," when He blessed me with a nice customer on the line. Or, when faced with an angry customer's rant, I'd press the mute button so I could ask the Lord for grace. In slow moments, I'd recite portions of Scripture to cement them in my memory.

> I had more than I ever dreamed of having; I was living the American dream. So why was I unhappy?

After the American Idols Live tour ended, I moved out of my one-bedroom apartment and into a three-bedroom house. I traded in my '96 Nissan with 135,000 miles on it for a shiny new 2007 Toyota Solara. I had more money in my bank account than I had ever had in my life. I had a record contract, a book contract, and a modeling contract. I was thankful for all those things, but something was missing, and for several weeks I couldn't understand what it was.

I had more than I ever dreamed of having. I was living the American dream. So why was I unhappy?

I finally realized the answer: Even though I had accumulated lots of *stuff,* my relationship with God had grown shallow. I'd stopped depending on Him. I had a hard time saying one word to God, let alone speaking to Him throughout my day. I struggled to open my Bible and couldn't imagine spending an hour searching the Scriptures for ways to be more like Jesus. And the very *thought* of getting up at five in the morning made me want to run and hide under my bed.

I had unknowingly traded fellowship with the Lord for the temporary pleasure of stuff. Instead of rising early to pray and read my Bible, I'd remained in my comfortable bedroom, secure in my new house. Instead of praying that my rattletrap vehicle would make it to the studio, I'd settled back in my Toyota and breathed in the lovely scent of a new car.

I began to feel distant from the Lord when I stopped spending consistent time with Him. My relationship with Jesus is like any other: As the girls in my Bible study reminded me, it requires time, honesty, and communication to grow.

In some ways I was richer living from paycheck to paycheck than I am now. But because God is a forgiving, loving, merciful Father, He will not let me go. He continues to pursue me, and when I forget Him, He makes me feel the void in my life.

I am thankful that He did not leave me in the place of being contented with worldly things. I could have easily ignored Him. I could have grown accustomed to the emptiness I felt inside. I could have spent the rest of my life missing the one thing that truly gives joy: a loving, intimate relationship with God.

Others Are Watching . . . All of Us

God has called me to this place, and He's placed you where you are. No matter where we are, others are watching our lives. Intimidating thought, isn't it?

I used to be intimidated by that thought, but since God is ordering my steps, I can trust that He will prepare and equip me to live out a Christian life before a secular world, no matter how tough it is.

It's easy to talk the Christian talk with other believers; we understand the same words and concepts, and we are bound together by the same Spirit. But when I speak of spiritual things to people who don't know the Lord, sometimes my words are taken as sheer foolishness. I have to be careful and pray for discretion, for Jesus Himself warned us not to give what is holy to unholy people.

Fame has put me on a tightrope of sorts, and I have to be careful to walk in a way that pleases God and allows me to be myself. I am certainly not a perfect person, and like most people, I'm not exactly thrilled with the idea of presenting my imperfections to the world. I'd love to be able to stand in front of a national audience and say, "Look at me! I'm an example of the victory you can achieve when you trust God completely!"

But—and I'm being honest here—I don't know that any of us can claim total victory in this life. We may accomplish certain goals or achieve victories along the way, but none of us is finished until we have run the entire course the Lord sets before us.

The author of Hebrews puts it this way:

> Since we are surrounded by such a huge crowd of
> witnesses to the life of faith, let us strip off every

weight that slows us down, especially the sin that so easily hinders our progress. And let us run with endurance the race that God has set before us. We do this by keeping our eyes on Jesus, on whom our faith depends from start to finish.

So take a new grip with your tired hands and stand firm on your shaky legs. Mark out a straight path for your feet. Then those who follow you, though they are weak and lame, will not stumble and fall but will become strong. (Hebrews 12:1-2, 12-13)

I love, love, *love* that passage because it says so much to me in my struggle with food. Having been exposed on national television as a person with a weight problem, I realize that the Lord has called me to be an example for other people who struggle with the same thing. I'm not an example of someone who has completely conquered; I'm someone who is going through it and can hold the hand of someone else going through it.

I am surrounded by a great crowd of witnesses—on earth and in the heavenly places—and I have to strip off the weight hindering my progress. For me, the *weight* is not only literal pounds but also those deep problems that spurred my food addiction in the first place. Through counseling and

219

prayer I am going to confront the hurts of my past and lay them to rest. I am going to turn them over to Jesus, who knows what pain is. He knows how suffering hurts. He has tasted shame and humiliation; He watched His friends desert Him in His hour of need.

No matter what you or I have been through, Jesus knows our pain. And He bore it, Scripture tells us, because of the joy He knew would be His afterward (see Hebrews 12:2).

Struggling with your addiction, whatever it is, won't be easy—nothing worth doing ever is. But the victory that follows will be worth the struggle.

True Beauty

I sometimes think about the sweet lady who e-mailed me to tell me I was the most beautiful person she'd ever seen. When I first read her message, I groaned—and wondered whether maybe she needed glasses. Now I am humbled by such words and realize that I've been blessed to be in a position to show the world what true beauty is. It's not external, but when it's *internal,* the light of God's loveliness shines through.

In the Old Testament, the Lord's favor is referred to as His "beauty." The psalmist wrote:

> *Let the beauty of the LORD our God be upon us,*
> *And establish the work of our hands for us;*
> *Yes, establish the work of our hands.*

PSALM 90:17 (NKJV)

Isaiah recorded God's promise to exchange His people's ashes of mourning for "a crown of beauty" (Isaiah 61:3), and described the Lord as a "glorious crown" (Isaiah 28:5). The New

Testament urges those who follow Jesus to live lives that will adorn the teachings of our Savior and make the Good News attractive to those who don't believe (see Titus 2:10).[4]

During my first interview after I'd made it to the top twenty-four, the reporter remarked that I was a role model for heavy women. Another writer referred to me as a Christian role model.

I don't take comments like those too much to heart because they're just words. What I do know for certain is that God's plan is for me to live for Him. He has called me to obedience, holiness, and transparency. But you know what? I believe He's calling you to do the same.

Wherever you are, whatever your "public," He's inviting you to walk with Jesus. Whether you walk in front of a lot of people or only in front of your children, don't let anyone diminish the importance of what you've been called to do. You can walk in beauty if you walk in obedience. You can walk in the light of God's favor.

No matter what your size or shape, it's important to be content with who you are. It's essential for believers to realize that our confidence comes from the Lord, not from our appearance.

Was Jesus beautiful? Perhaps no one has ever better represented the ideal of internal beauty, but though I know He has eyes filled with love, gentle hands, and a voice that thrills my soul, Scripture says that "there was nothing beautiful or majestic about his appearance, nothing to attract us to him" (Isaiah 53:2).

> No matter what your size or shape, it's important to be content with who you are. It's essential for believers to realize that our confidence comes from the Lord, not from our appearance.

Your external appearance should be the frame that enhances the beauty found inside you—the beauty that comes from knowing and following Jesus.

As Peter wrote, "Don't be concerned about the outward beauty. . . . You should clothe yourselves instead with the beauty that comes from within, the unfading beauty of a gentle and quiet spirit, which is so precious to God" (1 Peter 3:3-4).

Looking back to the time when I read that e-mail sent by the encouraging woman, I can see that because of the darkness I was in, I was not able to see truth.

Hidden in the Cleft of the Rock

In Exodus 33 we find the story of Moses' bold request to see the glorious presence of God. God replied, "'You may not look directly at my face, for no one may see me and live.' The LORD continued, 'Look, stand near me on this rock. As my glorious presence passes by, I will hide you in the crevice of the rock and cover you with my hand until I have passed by. Then I will remove my hand and let you see me from behind'" (Exodus 33:20-23).

So God covered Moses with His hand as His awesome glory passed by. Moses waited in darkness until God removed His sheltering hand, and then Moses could look out and see where God had been. Even the remnant of glory, however, was so powerful that Moses' face glowed after having witnessed it.

During my summer of depression, I lived in the darkness of despair. But God's hand sheltered me even there, and now that I've stepped out of the cleft of the rock, I can see where God has been. I hope the wonder of it all will radiate throughout the rest of my life.

There are things I wish I had done differently in that dark

time. As Moses waited in the dark, I'm sure he must have known he would eventually step into the light. I, on the other hand, refused to think about the future. The Father wanted me to crawl onto His lap so He could comfort me, but I resisted.

I wish I had found the courage to have a praise party. I could have worshipped my way out of that funk. With David, I could have said, "Unseal my lips, O Lord, that my mouth may praise you" (Psalm 51:15).

But now I am thankful that I missed the mark, because I can encourage you to learn from my mistakes.

At this point of my journey I can see that God has used everything—from my job at LifeWay to singing at Beth Moore events and competing in *American Idol*—to prepare me for what I'm doing today. I couldn't have designed a better education program for my unique ministry if I had tried. God is using all of those experiences, even the hard things like my groping for answers and questioning who He is.

I know a lot of people question God and His sovereignty. Is faith simply accepting what God does as inevitable, or is it believing God for specific things?

It's both. I believe God works with us as free moral agents even though He is sovereign over all of His creation. He created us, with our gifts and flaws, and our lives are a training ground where we learn lessons we will carry into eternity.

I believe God allowed me to endure months of darkness so I can assure you that light lives outside the cleft.

God doesn't call us to be comfortable, nor does He allow His children to run the show. Nowhere in His Word does He promise us an easy road; in fact, He tells us to take up our cross and follow Him. He also assures us that His grace is sufficient and His power is made perfect in our weakness.

A Tapestry Needs Light *and* Dark

Some people find it hard to believe that God's plan for us might include struggle and suffering. They want to believe that God wants us to always be happy, healthy, and prosperous—even rich! But though some of His children do seem to enjoy those blessings, I believe God sends all of His children through trials for a reason: He wants us to mature, to learn to call on Him, and to learn to trust Him in even the darkest hours of our lives.

Bible teacher Harold Willmington has compiled a list of reasons why God allows His children to suffer. The following is not an exhaustive list, but now that I stand on the other side of what felt to me like my own dark night of the soul, I can certainly relate to each of these points.

Sometimes God's children are allowed to struggle or suffer

- *to produce the fruit of patience in us:* "We can rejoice, too, when we run into problems and trials, for we know that they help us develop endurance" (Romans 5:3).
- *to produce the fruit of joy:* "His anger lasts only a moment, but his favor lasts a lifetime! Weeping may last through the night, but joy comes with the morning" (Psalm 30:5).
- *to produce the fruit of maturity:* "In his kindness God called you to share in his eternal glory by means of Christ Jesus. So after you have suffered a little while, he will restore, support, and strengthen you, and he will place you on a firm foundation" (1 Peter. 5:10).
- *to produce the fruit of righteousness:* "No discipline is enjoyable while it is happening—it's painful! But afterward there will be a peaceful harvest of right living for those who are trained in this way" (Hebrews 12:11).

- *to silence the evil one:* "Satan replied to the LORD, 'Yes, but Job has good reason to fear God. You have always put a wall of protection around him and his home and his property. You have made him prosper in everything he does. Look how rich he is! But reach out and take away everything he has, and he will surely curse you to your face!' 'All right, you may test him,' the LORD said to Satan. 'Do whatever you want with everything he possesses, but don't harm him physically.' So Satan left the LORD's presence" (Job 1:9-12).
- *to teach us:* "I used to wander off until you disciplined me; but now I closely follow your word" (Psalm 119:67).
- *to purify our lives:* [The Lord says,] "I will raise my fist against you. I will melt you down and skim off your slag. I will remove all your impurities" (Isaiah 1:25). "I have refined you, but not as silver is refined. Rather, I have refined you in the furnace of suffering" (Isaiah 48:10).
- *to make us like Christ:* "I want to know Christ and experience the mighty power that raised him from the dead. I want to suffer with him, sharing in his death, so that one way or another I will experience the resurrection from the dead!" (Philippians 3:10-11).
- *to glorify God:* "Call on me when you are in trouble, and I will rescue you, and you will give me glory" (Psalm 50:15).
- *to make us confess when we sin:* "Come, let us return to the LORD. He has torn us to pieces; now he will heal us. He has injured us; now he will bandage our wounds" (Hosea 6:1).

- *to reveal ourselves to ourselves:* "I take back everything I said, and I sit in dust and ashes to show my repentance" (Job 42:6).
- *to become an example to others:* "In everything we do, we show that we are true ministers of God. We patiently endure troubles and hardships and calamities of every kind. We have been beaten, been put in prison, faced angry mobs, worked to exhaustion, endured sleepless nights, and gone without food. We prove ourselves by our purity, our understanding, our patience, our kindness, by the Holy Spirit within us, and by our sincere love" (2 Corinthians 6:4-6).
- *to qualify us as counselors:* "Be happy with those who are happy, and weep with those who weep" (Romans 12:15).
- *to further the gospel witness:* "I want you to know, my dear brothers and sisters, that everything that has happened to me here has helped to spread the Good News" (Philippians 1:12).
- *to make us more than conquerors:* "Can anything ever separate us from Christ's love? Does it mean he no longer loves us if we have trouble or calamity, or are persecuted, or hungry, or destitute, or in danger, or threatened with death? . . . No, despite all these things, overwhelming victory is ours through Christ, who loved us" (Romans 8:35, 37).
- *to prepare us for a greater ministry:* "I tell you the truth, unless a kernel of wheat is planted in the soil and dies, it remains alone. But its death will produce many new kernels—a plentiful harvest of new lives" (John 12:24).

- *to prepare us for the coming Kingdom of God:*
  "If we endure hardship, we will reign with him"
  (2 Timothy 2:12).
- *to show the sovereignty of God:* "You have tested us,
  O God; you have purified us like silver. You captured us
  in your net and laid the burden of slavery on our backs.
  . . . We went through fire and flood, but you brought us
  to a place of great abundance (Psalm 66:10-12).[5]

Give God Your Dreams

At one point in my dark summer of 2006, if someone had asked
me whether I'd audition for *Idol* again, I'd have said no, the
experience wasn't worth it. But if you asked me today, I'd say
yes, definitely yes. *American Idol*—with its incredible highs and
lows—was part of God's plan for my life.

Amazing, isn't it, that God could use something as frivolous
as an entertainment-oriented television show to mold the life
of one of His children? Yet God can use *anything* to accomplish
His purposes. He is the Creator, and we are the creatures.

I am thirty years old—which, depending on your perspective, may be very old or very young! At thirty, however, I have
realized that I have much to learn about God, and I *needed* the
highs and lows of my *American Idol* adventure to prepare for
the future.

If I am to fully realize the dreams God and I are dreaming
together, I need to be able to handle the dark nights of the soul
as well as the sweet hours of praise and worship. I need to know
that God is as present in the darkness as He is in the brightness
of a happy day.

If you have buried a dream you thought God wanted for
you, dig it up. But know that your plan may or may not be part

of God's plan, so you'll have to come to the point where you're okay with that.

At the beginning of my *Idol* journey, I asked the Lord to use me—then I complained about how I was being used. That's a little like a teakettle complaining because it's set on a hot flame, isn't it? Our dreams are so personal that failure can result in a real sense of hopelessness. But there's always hope.

> At the beginning of my *Idol* journey, I asked the Lord to use me . . . then I complained about how I was being used.

Joseph had dreams. He dreamed that his bundle of grain stood up and his brothers' bundles bowed down to him. He was astute enough to realize that such a dream meant one day he would have power over his brothers. You probably remember that his brothers didn't take very kindly to his interpretation of the dream.

Later he dreamed that the sun, moon, and eleven stars bowed down to him. This time even his father was annoyed by the thought that he might one day bow before his son. And the brothers grew even more irritated—irritated enough that they sold Joseph into slavery and watched traders drag him off into the sunset, toward Egypt. Years passed, and Joseph grew to maturity in a strange land. While in Egypt, he served as a slave, was wrongly imprisoned, and finally rose to a position of prominence in Pharaoh's court. Thirteen years passed before his unusual dreams came true: Because of a dire famine in the land, his brothers entered Egypt to buy food. They were escorted to Joseph's palace, where they bowed low and gazed at a stranger in an Egyptian wig. They did not recognize their long-lost brother at all.

After several tests of his brothers' loyalty, Joseph finally revealed himself to them. "Don't be angry with yourselves for selling me to this place. It was God who sent me here ahead of you to preserve your lives" (Genesis 45:5) "You intended to harm me, but God intended it all for good. He brought me to this position so I could save the lives of many people" (Genesis 50:20).

So go ahead and dream big dreams for God. You can believe that He will honor your willingness to move forward on the Kingdom's behalf: "Seek the Kingdom of God above all else, and live righteously, and he will give you everything you need" (Matthew 6:33).

If you seek God and not what you want—don't seek His *hand,* but His *face*—He will equip you with everything you need. But God has to be your first priority. You can't have an idol; you can't idolize fame, fortune, success, or self-fulfillment. *God* has to be the object of your worship and passion.

The Power of Prayer

One of the things I learned though my time of struggle is the power of intercessory prayer. My praying friends—Dave, Cheryl, Chandra, Tammy, Kevin, Alicia, Fiona, Michael, Travis, Angela, Jennifer, Chance, and countless others—called and wrote and visited often, each time assuring me that their love for me was unconditional. They didn't love me because I had been on *American Idol*—they loved me because I was Mandisa, with all my insecurities and hang-ups.

Privately and in small groups, they prayed for me. They helped me sort things out by talking to me and listening to my struggles. They prayed me out the door when I went to California, and they prayed me back to life when I came home.

My praying friends have taught me to pray for others. Life

equals time, so by investing my time in prayers for others, I am investing my life in their ministries, their families, their eternal destinies. When I pray for my fellow *Idol* contestants and the *Idol* staff (including Simon!), I am making an eternal investment in their lives.

Jesus prayed for others. He prayed for Simon Peter and even for the soldiers who gambled for His robe at the foot of the cross (see Luke 22:32; 23:34). We also are to pray for those who persecute us (see Matthew 5:44).

Paul admonished us to be intercessors in prayer: "I urge you, first of all, to pray for all people. Ask God to help them; intercede on their behalf, and give thanks for them. Pray this way for kings and all who are in authority so that we can live peaceful and quiet lives marked by godliness and dignity" (1 Timothy 2:1-2).

I am asking the Lord to do great things through my *Idol* friends and my dear intercessors. I see far too many Christians living a "safe" Christian life, never daring to imagine or dream of anything more than the ordinary. But we serve a great God who is capable of great things!

I love the latter part of Daniel 11:32 in the King James Version: "The people that do know their God shall be strong, and do exploits."

Who? The people who know their God.

What will they be? They will be strong.

What will they *do?* Exploits. They will resist the evil one and perform notable and heroic acts.

If you're walking with the Lord, life should be exciting! I don't think it's possible to live a humdrum life if you're putting your faith in Jesus. Walking with Him is a constant thrill. That doesn't mean you have to be jet-setting around the globe every day, because you can have a nine-to-five job *and* a whirlwind life with the Lord.

When I get to heaven, I don't want to stand before the judgment seat of Christ and hear, "You did a decent job, but you should have trusted Me more and praised Me more often." I want to hear Jesus say, "You believed Me, you trusted Me, and you didn't hold anything back."

Christianity is not about rules and restrictions. True Christianity is centered on a relationship with Jesus, and it's never boring. Some people paint the Christian life in terms of going to church on Sunday and not doing this or that, but God can't be boxed in with a list of behaviors.

Life with Jesus is an amazing ride. Beth Moore always says, "There ain't no high like the Most High," and I agree absolutely. No drug, no alcohol, no food can match the excitement I feel when I'm walking with the Lord. There is no feeling as satisfying as being in the center of His will.

Looking toward the Future

What does the future hold for me? I don't know—and I'm *excited* that I don't know. I do know I'll be recording an album with EMI Christian Music Group, and I've also signed with the Ashley Stewart clothing company to be a model. That is my favorite clothing store, so I'll be doing a few appearances at store openings where I can sign pictures and hug people who stop by.

In the coming months I'm going to continue to work on my

food addiction. My love for food is, in a sense, my "thorn in the flesh," the flaw God allows to keep me humble and dependent on Him. I will probably always love the taste of hot apple pie and ice cream, but I'm going to place my love for God—and my commitment to maintaining a healthy temple for the Spirit— above my need to indulge my appetite. I'd welcome the opportunity to speak to and work with people who are also struggling with food-related addictions ranging from overeating to bulimia or anorexia. Safety often comes in numbers, and I figure we can conquer our food problems together.

The Lord has called me to encourage the body of Christ, so since leaving the tour I have sung at several churches and Christian conferences. But because the Lord has also called me to represent Him to people who don't know Him, I have performed at places like the historic Apollo Theater in New York and for the Walt Disney World Christmas Day Parade in Orlando.

I welcome opportunities to sing for secular events because I enjoy meeting all types of people and don't want to close myself off from anyone.

There are, however, certain things I wouldn't feel comfortable doing. As I told *The Advocate,* I don't think I'd feel comfortable singing at an event organized by a homosexual group—or any group, for that matter, that promotes activities that run contrary to my beliefs.

Because I believe God wants me to live a life of holiness on and off the platform, I won't swear or take the Lord's name in vain in a performance. I won't talk or sing about things that don't conform with my beliefs.

But I enjoy singing fun, celebratory songs like "I'm Every Woman"—I began every night of the tour with that song, then followed it by dedicating "If I Were Your Woman" to Ruben

Studdard. My set concluded with me singing "I'm Your Angel" with Ace.

Before I brought Ace onto the stage to join me, I would take a moment to speak to the concert attendees. I would explain that there were better singers who could be on that stage, but the reason I stood before them was because a big God had big plans for me. I would encourage them by saying that the same God had a purpose for them, too. I would exhort them to dream *big*, because God is able to do more than they could ever ask, think, or imagine.

I knew the girls were waiting to squeal when Ace walked out onto the stage, but I hoped the words I spoke would somehow stick with them. Time after time, I was sent notes from mothers in the audience who wanted to thank me for saying what I did.

I long for those kinds of opportunities. One of my goals is for people to see that Christians are regular people. I loved dancing to "I'm Every Woman." I really *do* have a crush on Ruben Studdard, but I also know that God is real. He is fun! Why else would He invent laughter? Why else would He create *giraffes?* He enjoys knowing that I enjoy my life with Him.

When I sing in front of secular audiences and hear things like "You are so beautiful" or "You have such a presence," I use those compliments as opportunities to share where my beauty and presence really come from—the Lord!

I know it can be difficult to stay grounded when you achieve

One of my goals is for people to see that Christians are regular people. I loved dancing to "I'm Every Woman." I really *do* have a crush on Ruben Studdard, but I also know that God is real.

earthly success, but I know where my gifts and opportunities originate. I also know where I would be if it had not been for the Lord: either in bed with the covers drawn over my head or on the sofa eating a bag of popcorn with extra butter!

I am always humbled when God shows me how my obedience has touched lives. When a mom approaches me with her teenager and whispers confidentially, "Thank you for being a role model to my daughter," I am thrilled. When a woman passes me a note on an airplane and says I have a wonderful understanding of forgiveness, I want to fall to my knees in thanksgiving.

In 2 Corinthians 1:3-4, Paul wrote, "All praise to God, the Father of our Lord Jesus Christ. God is our merciful Father and the source of all comfort. He comforts us in all our troubles so that we can comfort others. When they are troubled, we will be able to give them the same comfort God has given us."

Even with all my struggles, *American Idol* really was worth it. God turned my misery into ministry by allowing me to comfort others.

On the season-five finale, I stood with the other top-twelve contestants and sang Barry Manilow's "I Made It through the Rain." As I looked around the stage at the faces that had become so dear to me, I renewed my vow to pray for those folks for the rest of my life.

I am so thankful for the friends the Lord has brought into my life. I am grateful for the doors He has opened, but I am just as appreciative for the doors He has purposely and lovingly closed. I know beyond a shadow of a doubt that God's will for me is perfect.

The apostle John wrote of the time when Jesus began to wash his disciples' feet at their last supper together. Peter, horrified that their master would stoop to do the work of a servant, tried to stop Jesus.

Jesus looked up at him and said, "You don't understand now what I am doing, but someday you will" (John 13:7).

I entered the world on October 2, 1976. Now I smile when I think of how the Lord ordered the first three decades of my life. I have traveled from obscurity to dizzying heights; I have received praise and scorn in equal measure. I've been admired and mocked; I've been loved and hated. I've been too overjoyed for words and too depressed to get out of bed.

But through it all, God has proven Himself faithful. As I travel the rest of my life journey, I know there will be situations where I don't fully comprehend what God is doing. I may feel pain—even grief—but I've learned this: One day I will understand. That day may come later in this life or it may wait until I sit in a heavenly movie theater with my Savior.

Until then, even though I may not always see clearly, I will trust Jesus as He guides me down the path He has prepared for me.

If I may paraphrase something I once told a national television audience: This book goes out to everybody who wants to be free. Your addiction, lifestyle, or situation may be big, but God is bigger.

Trust me. I know.

NOTES

CHAPTER 1: WAITING PATIENTLY

1. "Media Use and Obesity among Children," National Institute on Media and the Family, http://www.mediafamily.org/facts/facts_tvandobchild.shtml.
2. Paul Lee Tan, *Encyclopedia of 7700 Illustrations: A Treasury of Illustrations, Anecdotes, Facts and Quotations for Pastors, Teachers and Christian Workers* (Garland, Tex.: Bible Communications, 1996), electronic version.
3. Rufus Matthew Jones, quoted in *The Encyclopedia of Religious Quotations*, ed. Frank S. Mead (Old Tappan, N.J.: Revell, 1965), 479.

CHAPTER 3: A NEW SONG

1. Henry T. Blackaby and Claude V. King, *Experiencing God—Knowing and Doing the Will of God* (Nashville: LifeWay, 1990). The seven realities are listed on the inside back cover.

CHAPTER 4: THE JOY OF TRUSTING

1. Darrell Evans, "Trading My Sorrows," Hosanna! Music (Mobile, Ala.: Integrity, 1998).

CHAPTER 5: TENDER MERCIES

1. Donna de la Cruz, "FTC Fines Diet Drug Marketers," *The Tampa Tribune*, January 5, 2007, B-1.
2. Angela Elwell Hunt and Laura Krauss Calenberg, *Beauty from the Inside Out* (Nashville: Nelson, 1993), 159.
3. http://www.wonderquest.com/size-women-us.htm.
4. *Women's Health Matters* newsletter, summer 2001, found at http://ucsfhealth.org/adult/pubs/whm/nwlssummer2001.pdf.
5. Garance Franke-Ruta, "The Natural Beauty Myth," *Wall Street Journal*, December 15, 2006, W17.

CHAPTER 9: LOSING COURAGE

1. Stephen D. Eyre, *Drawing Close to God: The Essentials of a Dynamic Quiet Time* (Downers Grove, Ill.: InterVarsity, 1997), 86.
2. R. C. Sproul, *Chosen by God* (Carol Stream, Ill.: Tyndale House Publishers, 1996), 172.

CHAPTER 10: IN THE LORD'S THOUGHTS

1. Exodus 14:15-21.
2. Numbers 22:21-31.
3. Acts 20:7-12.
4. Walter A. Elwell and Philip Wesley Comfort, *Tyndale Bible Dictionary* (Carol Stream, Ill.: Tyndale, 2001), 155.
5. Harold L. Willmington, *Willmington's Book of Bible Lists* (Carol Stream, Ill.: Tyndale, 1987), electronic edition.

ABOUT THE AUTHORS

"I don't ever remember not singing," Mandisa once replied to an interviewer's question. Mentored by her high school music director, she began to learn the technical aspects of singing. After graduating from high school, Mandisa attended Fisk University, where she earned a bachelor's degree in music with a concentration in vocal performance. She did session work in Nashville for several years, and at twenty-eight she auditioned for the fifth season of the reality television show *American Idol*, where she made it all the way to the top ten before being eliminated. Her powerful voice, musical versatility, and strong faith made her a standout contestant and have earned her the respect of peers and viewers alike. When Mandisa isn't on the road, she lives in Nashville, Tennessee.

Christy Award winner Angela Hunt writes books for readers who have learned to expect the unexpected. With more than three million copies of her books sold worldwide, she is the best-selling author of *The Tale of Three Trees, The Note, Unspoken,* and more than one hundred other titles.

She and her youth pastor husband make their home in Florida with their mastiffs. One of their dogs was featured on *Live with Regis and Kelly* as the second-largest canine in America.

Readers may visit her Web site at www.angelahuntbooks.com.